MORE TORAH THERAPY

FURTHER REFLECTIONS ON
THE WEEKLY SIDRAH AND SPECIAL OCCASIONS

MORE TORAH THERAPY

FURTHER REFLECTIONS ON
THE WEEKLY SIDRAH AND SPECIAL OCCASIONS

by

Rabbi Reuven P. Bulka

KTAV PUBLISHING HOUSE, INC.
HOBOKEN, N.J.

Copyright © 1993
Reuven P. Bulka
Library of Congress Cataloging-in-Publication Data

Bulka, Reuven P.
    More Torah therapy : further reflections on the weekly sidrah and special occasions / by Reuven P. Bulka.
    p.   cm.
    Includes indexes.
    ISBN 0-88125-464-9
    1. Bible. O.T. Pentateuch--Sermons. 2. Jewish sermons, English--Canada. I. Title.
BS1225.4.B83 1993
296.4'2--dc20   93-13931
                                                            CIP

Manufactured in the United States of America
KTAV Publishing House, Inc., 900 Jefferson St., Hoboken, NJ 07030

For

Yisroel Meir and Dovid Nisson

*First Fruits
of our
First Fruits*

TABLE OF CONTENTS

INTRODUCTION 1

BERESHIT—Beginning from the Beginning 3
NOAH—For His Generations..6
LEKH LEKHA—The Godly Way...9
VA-YERA—Looking Back...11
HAYYEI SARAH—Falling, or Rising, in Love 13
TOLEDOT—A Blessing Must Be Deserved..........................15
VA-YEZE—Double Standards of Morality 18
VA-YISHLAH—Prayer Perspective 21
VA-YESHEV—Rising to the Challenge 23
MI-KEZ—Folly of Hate 25
VA-YIGGASH—The Transcendent Ingredient
   in Parenthood 27
VA-YEHI—Equal but Fair 29
SHEMOT—Justifiable Skepticism 32
VA-ERA—Vigor of Old Age 34
BO—A Matter of Principle 36
BE-SHALLAH—Eternal War 39
YITRO—Humble Deservedness 41
MISHPATIM—Her Time...43
TERUMAH—Higher Religiosity 46
TEZAVVEH—Ordinary and Extraordinary............................48
KI TISSA—Unity for the Right Reasons 50
VA-YAKHEL—Keeping Your Word, Your Thought 52
PEKUDEI—Neatness Counts..55
VA-YIKRA—Divulging Painful Truths 57
ZAV—Thinking Big 59
SHEMINI—When Kindness Isn't 61

TAZRI'A — Why the Eighth Day? 63
MEZORA — Why the Hyssop? 66
AHAREI MOT — Nothing New under the Sun 69
KEDOSHIM — As Yourself 72
EMOR — Why Not a Divorcee 74
BE-HAR — Making Everything Count 76
BE-HUKKOTAI — Cause and Effect 79
BE-MIDBAR — Levitic Demographics 82
NASO — We Are Capable 84
BE-HA'ALOTKHA — Capsule History 86
SHELAH — Israel as an Emotion 89
KORAH — No More Defense 92
HUKKAT — The Red Heifer Paradox 94
BALAK — Hate and Envy 96
PINHAS — True Pioneers 98
MATTOT — Built-in Protection 100
MASEI — Honorable Mention 103
DEVARIM — Dimensions of Leadership 105
VA-ETHANNAN — Conditional Destiny 108
EKEV — Land of Opportunity 111
RE'EH — Constructive Response 113
SHOFETIM — Leadership — Ins and Outs 116
KI TEZE — Maintaining the Sources 118
KI TAVO — Roots of Thanksgiving 120
NIZAVIM — Down to Earth 123
VA-YELEKH — The Unity Legacy 125
HA'AZINU — The Old and the New 128
VE-ZOT HA-BERAKHAH — Uplifting Torah 131
ROSH HA-SHANAH
    Water, Water, Everywhere 134
    The *Akeda* — a Test within a Test 137
YOM KIPPUR
    Guilt Trip — Worthwhile Journey 140
    Collective Guilt 143
PESAH
    What If? 146

Questions and the Questioner 149
SHAVUOT
A Fair Hearing 152
Forced to Choose 154
SUKKOT
To Have ... To Be 157
Religion as an Antidepressant 159
SHEMINI ATZERET-SIMḤAT TORAH
The Route to Our Roots 161
ZAKHOR and PARAH
Remembering What We Would Like to Forget 164
ḤANUKKAH—Balanced Perspective 167
PURIM—Is Purim Modeled after Pesaḥ? 169

IN-DEPTH STUDIES

THE SELLING OF THE BIRTHRIGHT
Making Sense of a Perplexing Episode 175
REACTION TO TERROR—A Biblical Perspective 181
THE RATIONALE FOR SACRIFICE
A Postscript on Abravanel's Defense of Rambam 186

APPLICABILITY INDEX 193
SUBJECT INDEX 197

INTRODUCTION

A number of years ago, my first collection of thoughts for the weekly Torah readings and special occasions appeared. It was entitled *Torah Therapy*. The title was not meant to suggest that this was a book about psychology and Judaism, as was clearly indicated in the subtitle, *Reflections on the Weekly Sedra and Special Occasions*.

Nevertheless, there were some who complained that they were misled by the title. To them, I apologize. Because of them, I seriously debated whether to abandon that title for this, my second book of thoughts on the weekly readings and special occasions. After serious deliberation, I decided, for the sake of continuity, and since most people appreciated the original title, to call this volume *More Torah Therapy*.

Perhaps even more than the first volume, this book touches on so many aspects of human interaction—with God, with other people, with one's self. It is, like it or not, therapy straight from the Torah, therapy of a directive, affirmative, positive nature.

In this volume I have added a new feature, what I call the Applicability Index. It lists the applicability of the presentations to other occasions in a way which I hope will make the book even more useful.

Only a few of the pieces in this book have been previously published. The in-depth studies at the end of the volume originally appeared in *Dor L'Dor*, and I thank its editor, Dr. Shimon Bakon, for his permission to reprint them. Thanks also to the Rabbinical Council of America, and its Executive Vice-

President, Rabbi Binyomin Walfish, for permission to reprint some pieces that originally appeared in the RCA Sermon Manual.

The material in this volume was inspired by my beloved congregation, Machzikei Hadas, in Ottawa, where I have been privileged to serve for over twenty-five years. I warmly acknowledge my appreciation to them even as they wonder why these presentations are so short.

To Blanche Osterer, who put so much of this down on computer from barely intelligible dictation, goes my kudos for her talent and her patience.

As always, my wife, ever busy and overworked, still found time to proofread the book. This acknowledgment is just a fraction of the thanks I owe to her.

To Manny Singer, who made my task so much easier through his vast knowledge of computers and his continuing eagerness to help, goes my profound gratitude.

Finally, my appreciation to Bernard Scharfstein of KTAV, for his confidence in this book, and his special efforts to assure its publication.

>Reuven P. Bulka
>Ottawa, Ontario
>Shevat, 5753
>February, 1993

SIDRAH BERESHIT
Beginning from the Beginning

The Torah begins from the beginning. The first words of the Torah describe the creation of the world and its inhabitants, up to and including the creation of the first human being. This is the way it should be, or at least so we would assume. However, the first comment by Rashi on the Torah questions whether the Torah should have begun from the beginning of the creation of the world (Bereshit 1:1). Rashi, in his indispensable commentary to the Torah, asserts that the Torah should have started with the words "This month shall be for you the beginning of months; it shall be the first month of the year for you" (Shemot 12:2). This is a more desirable beginning, since it is the first commandment through which the Israelite community was itself commanded into existence as a faith community, says Rashi.

If that is the case, then why indeed does the Torah begin from the beginning? The answer given by Rashi is that by beginning from the beginning, from creation itself, we are able to respond to a claim that may be made against us, Israel, by the nations of the world. They may accuse Israel of taking away the land from the seven nations. We answer that all land belongs to God. God created the world and gave the land to whomever God desired. It was because God so desired it that the seven nations inhabited Israel, and it was because God so willed it that the land was later given to the people of Israel.

Needless to say, this comment by Rashi, coming at the opening of his outstanding commentary to the Torah, is quite problematic.

What bothers Rashi at the very outset? Why does he ask the question, and what is the nature of the response?

It may be possible to read into Rashi a basic statement about the Judaic approach to life and to the world. Rashi addresses himself to a very simple question: Should we think in universal terms, or should we think in parochial terms? Should we be concerned about the world in its totality, or should we be preoccupied with the immediate environment, with the Jewish community in which we are housed?

Rashi begins with the assumption that since the Torah is for Israel, it should begin with the commandments that have made Israel the unique faith community that it is. This is the question: Why indeed does the Torah not begin with the first commandment that effectively commanded Israel into existence?

The response of Rashi does not speak in broad philosophical terms about universality and global responsibility; it strikes instead at the heart of Israel's relationship to the world at large. The first sentence of the Torah is an answer to an anticipated charge that may be leveled against the Israelite community. We may be charged with grand theft, theft of someone else's land. The sense of anticipation in Rashi is uncanny, because this is precisely what has happened over the course of the last few decades.

The Torah begins with a statement which enables us to relate effectively to the world at large. Rashi clearly argues that our concerns, although they must relate to our immediate environment, must always be in the context of the greater responsibility of the community of Israel to the world at large. We have an obligation to maintain our credibility as a faith community not only in our eyes, but in the eyes of the world. We cannot take the attitude that whatever is said about us by others is meaningless and we can therefore safely ignore it. We do not have an obligation to convert the entire world to Judaism. But we are obligated to spread the values of the Torah to the entire world community so that the practice of morals and ethics that is underlined in the Torah may become universal. Without credibility, this cannot occur.

It is for this reason that the Torah begins with creation. God appears immediately as the creator of the world, not as the parochial God of a people. And this is the substance of the answer that we give to the nations who will accuse Israel. It is true that the Land of Israel had been inhabited by the seven nations; we admit that. But we add that the seven nations were there as tenants of God's property. We too, in going into Israel, are tenants of God's property.

We do not have any claim to the real estate of Israel that is more basic than the fact God told us this is our home and engineered our coming into our home. For a while there were other tenants, then it was given to us as a permanent home. We were thrust out of it into exile, but with the promise that there would be a return to the home, a return which has taken hold in our time. We are partners in the unfolding of God's plan, a plan which includes not only the ultimate destiny of the Israelite community, but of the world at large. This comes through quite clearly in the fact that the first words of the Torah deal with the creation of the world.

Thus, this comment by Rashi, the very first of his comments on the Torah, serves to create the foundation for global concern that must be the hallmark of Jewish existence.

SIDRAH NOAḤ
For His Generations

Noaḥ was a righteous man. He is given this worthy title by the Torah (Bereshit 6:9). He is also called complete (*tamim*), but that sense of completeness, attached as it is to his title of righteous (*zaddik*), is not necessarily an additional crown on Noaḥ's head.

Noaḥ was "complete in his generations" (Bereshit 6:9). According to one view in the Talmud, that of Resh Lakish, this means that he was righteous in the corrupt generation in which he lived, and how much more so would he have been righteous in other generations. However, another, and seemingly more frequently quoted view, that of Rabbi Yoḥanan, is that he was righteous in his generations, but not in other generations (Sanhedrin 108a). In other words, Noaḥ was righteous for his time, but is not in the same category as Avraham, Yizḥak, Yaakov, Mosheh, and Aharon.

This is the traditional understanding of the qualification that Noaḥ was "complete in his generations." However, there may be another sense conveyed by this description, which gives a slightly different context to the less laudatory view of Noaḥ.

From the time that Noaḥ was told about the impending deluge that was to engulf his corrupt generation, until the actual cataclysmic event, 120 years elapsed. Noaḥ went to great trouble building an elaborate Ark, which was to house adequate representation from all the species. Additionally, the Ark would have been open to anyone who desired to take this free cruise, should they have so opted.

It is a lamentable fact of that generation, that in all the time between the announcement of the impending flood, and the actual doom, Noaḥ was able to save no one, except his own family. The only human beings in the Ark were Noaḥ, his wife, his children, and their wives.

Ten generations later, when Avraham came on the scene, he too encountered a world that was corrupt, although it was a theological corruptness that infused Avraham's generation. Avraham went out of his way to attract individuals, to convince them of the folly of idolatry and the superiority of monotheism. It was not Avraham's desire to convert the world, since at that time there was no institutionalized belief system. Avraham simply desired to uplift individuals, to infuse them with a sense of meaningful connectedness to God. This would thereby improve their life in its spiritual quality, and thus also in its day-to-day activity.

Avraham's success came because he was convinced of the truth of monotheistic belief, and also because he was not satisfied with merely saving himself and his family. He realized that the stakes were too high, and that merely saving the family was not sufficient. After all, what value is there in saving your own family, if everyone else around you thinks differently, and behaves in a way that is threatening to the world's future.

Avraham realized that the strength of individual families is enhanced by improving the quality of all surrounding families, even though they may be totally unrelated. There was nothing that could stand in the way of Avraham sharing his worldview with others and hoping that they would respond to his intellectual challenge.

Noaḥ, on the other hand, did not aggressively pursue the "mending of the world." Satisfied that his family would be saved, he merely left the Ark door open in case anyone wanted to enter. There is no evidence that he actively searched out individuals to convince them that their corruptness would be their undoing, and to beg them to reject that course and become more morally sensitive.

In a word, Noaḥ was complete in his generations. Those generations that were his, namely himself and his children, he made sure would remain intact and complete (*tamim*). The generations of others, however, did not concern him as much.

It is this which is perhaps insinuated in the biblical description of Noaḥ as complete in his generations. It is nice that Noaḥ was responsible and that he undertook to save his family—and actually succeeded in doing so. But his family, and indeed the world, would have been much better off if the entire generation had been saved by being led to a more noble mode of existence.

Noaḥ did not achieve this. Hence, even though he was undoubtedly righteous, his was not the type of righteousness through which exalted world history is made. The Judaic ethos has always been more closely identified with the type of righteousness exemplified by Avraham: the sharing of universal values in a way that will better humankind. Noaḥ exemplified the attitude of being happy with one's self and family and isolating them from the rest of the world. We are, at the very root, children of Avraham, not children of Noaḥ.

SIDRAH LEKH LEKHA
The Godly Way

The very beginning of Lekh Lekha, innocent as it may seem, reveals much about the godly way. There is no mention of any precipitant episode. Suddenly, seemingly out of nowhere, God tells Avraham to go from his land, the place of his birth, and his father's house, to the land that God will show him (Bereshit 12:1).

The seemingly excessive precision concerning the place Avraham is to leave is startling in contrast with the imprecision concerning his destination. Avraham knew whence he was leaving. It would have made more sense for God to simply say "Go to the place which I [God] will identify." Instead, God conveys to Avraham great detail about the place he is leaving but says nothing about where Avraham is going.

The conclusion one reaches from this is that the main purpose of God's instruction was not that Avraham go someplace but that he leave a certain place. The main purpose was for Avraham to leave his parental home. Why?

Avraham could have stayed to continue his fight against idolatry, but this would have brought him into continual confrontation with his family, especially with Teraḥ, his father. Rather than having Avraham live in conflict with his parents, God tells him to take the peaceful route, to depart. By departing, Avraham can continue the battle against idolatry and at the same time avoid painful clashes with his parents. He can maintain respect and at the same time maintain his principles.

One would have thought that God would appear to Avraham and encourage him to continue the battle with his father, destroy the idols, and thereby win the battle for God. But that is not the godly way. God wanted Avraham to wage this ideological struggle, but not at the price of sacrificing moral principle, the moral principle of respecting one's parents.

This seemingly innocent beginning to the saga of Avraham is an eloquent testimony to the godly way, to the Jewish way. The Jewish way is not to seek battle, but to avoid it; not to embrace conflict, but to run away from it.

A little while later, when the shepherds of Avraham are locked in conflict with the shepherds of Lot, Avraham retreats from the fight. He tells Lot to choose any land he wants for grazing and that he, Avraham, will take what is left. Avraham had learned the lesson well, that it is crucial to avoid conflict.

But there are limits. When Lot is kidnapped, nothing stands in Avraham's way as he launches the battle to rescue Lot from captivity (Bereshit 14:14-16).

After the rescue, God appears to Avraham and tells him not to be afraid (Bereshit 15:1). What had Avraham done to be afraid? Avraham may have feared that he had killed unnecessarily in his successful effort to free Lot. This is further evidence of the sensitivity to moral responsibility exhibited by Avraham. Even in the legitimate struggle against oppressive adversaries, Avraham, who does not doubt the justice of his cause, is nevertheless afraid that he may have gone beyond his moral mandate.

It is this type of sensitivity to human life and godly values that is the hallmark of Avraham. It remains, to this very day, the prevailing concern as Israel continues its struggle to attain peace.

SIDRAH VA-YERA
Looking Back

In Israel, near the Dead Sea, there is a rock formation-pillar of salt which, when observed from a certain angle, resembles the contours of a woman, ostensibly the wife of Lot. The Torah reports that Lot's wife looked backward, and became a pillar of salt (Bereshit 19:26). This occurred during the hasty escape from the conflagration that engulfed Sedom, a city which heretofore had been the residence of Lot and his wife.

What exactly happened? What is meant by the statement that Lot's wife became a pillar of salt? Ibn Ezra's commentary suggests that Lot's wife was not transformed into a pillar of salt, but rather, that she was covered by salt layers. Thus the statement that she became a pillar of salt means that her human body became encased by salt.

This obviously makes the biblical description more intelligible. But what really happened to Lot's wife? Why did she look back? One may assume that Lot's wife looked back simply because she was reluctant to leave. She obviously loved Sedom and looked back with a sense of longing.

When she saw what was happening to her beloved place of residence, she probably became transfixed at the tragedy that was unfolding, and was rendered frozen, immobile, unable to move. This is somewhat similar to the sensation felt by a person who is crossing the street and suddenly sees a car approaching at top speed. The best thing to do in such a circumstance is to avoid the oncoming car, but often one becomes paralyzed with fear, unable to move. The person then does the worst thing: he or she remains in place.

The biblical report of what happened to Lot's wife is more than a mere footnote. One may assume that there is a moral lesson in what happened to her. With all the goings-on in Sedom, and the warning of its imminent destruction, Lot's wife should have come to the realization that the place was corrupt, that she had become corrupted in the years she had spent there. Given this opportunity to escape from Sedom and its immoral society, she should have run away as quickly as she could, without looking back. But even then, knowing all that she did, she could not wrestle free from the hold Sedom had on her. This was unfortunate; for Lot's wife, it became tragic.

The moral gently suggested is that there are occasions in our history, both personal and communal, when it is time to leave a country which is oppressive. When that time comes, and the opportunity beckons, one dare not look backward. One should take the opportunity to escape and run as quickly as possible to a safe haven.

In our generation, hundreds of thousands have learned the lesson of Lot's wife. They have improved their lot in life by running to the safe haven for every Jew, Israel, never looking back.

SIDRAH ḤAYYEI SARAH
Falling, or Rising, in Love

How to find the right life partner is a challenge that has faced humankind since the beginning of history. In Ḥayyei Sarah, much attention is given to the efforts of Avraham to find the proper wife for his son Yizḥak. He sends his trusted servant Eliezer on this mission, with strict instructions concerning who could be chosen, and who not (Bereshit 24:3-4).

It is a well-known story. Eliezer sets as his test for the suitability of a woman as Yizḥak's wife that the woman will offer to give drink not only to him (Eliezer) but to his camels as well.

It turns out that a young girl named Rivkah does exactly that. The difficulty then faced by Eliezer is convincing Rivkah's family to let the young girl return with him to Yizḥak. After much negotiation, the family finally agrees to let Rivkah go back with Eliezer to marry Yizḥak. The Torah language describing their union is fascinating. We are told that Yizḥak took Rivkah unto him, that she became his wife, and he then loved her (Bereshit 24:67).

Yizḥak, it seems, has it all backwards, or is it we that have it all backwards? Yizḥak obviously did not fall in love and then get married. He first got married, and then "fell" in love. The very words "falling in love" are themselves ominous. It would be much more appropriate to speak about rising in love. The choice of term may point to one of the major concerns in choosing a mate. If love is the primary focus, then the relationship is more likely to be a fall, since that love may merely be infatuation. Infatuation is usually not long-lasting, nor is it rooted in some strong spiritual link.

The girl that Yizḥak married was kind and considerate. She also shared many of the values that Yizḥak held dear. With this general framework of commonality and fundamental *mentschlichkeit*, it was only a matter of time before the relationship became more entrenched, and likeness of commitment became love for each other.

Perhaps the way of Yizḥak and Rivkah is indeed the better way. Perhaps the focus in setting out to find one's mate, is not merely to ask the question, Do I love this one or that one? Rather, the key question should be, Do we share enough, do we care enough, so that our relationship can grow in love rather than fall in it? Love is vital, but value sharing at once generates love and enhances the long-term prospects for the love to endure.

SIDRAH TOLEDOT
A Blessing Must Be Deserved

The dominant theme in Toledot is the confrontation between Yaakov and Esau. The confrontation begins after the death of Avraham, when Esau gives up the rights of the firstborn. It culminates when Yaakov apparently takes away the blessing that Yizḥak had reserved for Esau.

One can understand how individuals would fight over the rights of the firstborn. There is a tangible benefit—inheritance and other matters—to being the firstborn. But what is the purpose of fighting over a blessing? If a blessing is given on the basis of false assumptions, how can it ever become the blessing it is intended to be? Beyond this, if Rivkah and Yaakov were such firm believers, they should have trusted in God and not put so much stock in the blessing of Yizḥak. If God wants to bestow blessing, that blessing will be forthcoming.

In the continuing feud between Yaakov and Esau, more was at issue than just the question of who would receive Yizḥak's blessing. The crucial concern was the question of who would carry on the traditions of Avraham and Yizḥak. Who would be the model that people would relate to? Who would be the carrier of the norms and the values espoused originally by Avraham and carried on by Yizḥak? Who would be the Ambassador of Monotheism? Rivkah understood that if the blessing, which would then take the form of Yizḥak's stamp of approval, were bestowed upon Esau, it would spell disaster for her posterity, for Yizḥak's posterity. She therefore felt a sacred obligation to alert Yizḥak, even via subterfuge, to the fact that he had been deceived by his son.

Yizḥak assumed that Esau deserved to be the carrier of Abrahamic tradition. However, Esau was a clever individual who hid much from his father by being exceedingly respectful and mindful of even the slightest nuances in his father's presence. Behind his father's back, Esau was another person altogether. Rivkah, who had grown up in the house of the master of chicanery, Lavan, saw through her son Esau. Yizḥak, who saw only the purity of Avraham in his formative years, was totally oblivious to the fraud that was being perpetrated upon him.

Upon learning that Esau is about to be blessed, Rivkah urges Yaakov to dress up as his brother and present himself to his father as Esau. Yaakov is understandably anxious, but he nevertheless carries through this plan. He is blessed by Yizḥak, who assumes that he is blessing not Yaakov but Esau.

It is interesting to note that when Esau finally arrives, and Yizḥak realizes that he was fooled, Yizḥak does not take back the blessing that he had mistakenly bestowed upon Yaakov—he endorses that blessing (Bereshit 27:33). In other words, Yizḥak, rather than showering his wrath upon Yaakov, reinforces the blessing that he had originally given to him under false pretenses.

Why this reaction, instead of horror and rejection? We can logically assume that a running battle went on between Yizḥak and Rivkah as their twin sons were growing up. Rivkah probably complained to Yizḥak that Esau was misleading him, that Yaakov was indeed the individual to carry on Abrahamic tradition. Yizḥak, however, held his ground almost to the end. However, when he saw how easy it was for Yaakov to dress up as Esau, he realized how easy it must have been for Esau to dress up as Yaakov, as a very noble character. Suddenly, in a moment of great revelation, he saw the truth, the wisdom of all the arguments that had been projected by his wife. He therefore reinforced the blessing he had given to Yaakov.

The outgrowth of this entire episode is that Yaakov's blessing is not unconditional. It is a blessing based on deservedness, as it came from a tenuous circumstance. Only when Yaakov plays the role of Yaakov and lives up to the responsibilities as authentic carrier of tradition, can Yaakov expect that the blessing given will actually take hold.

In retrospect, perhaps this is ideal. It is certainly not healthy for any person or group to feel that they have a stranglehold on blessing and well-being, and a commensurate right to complain if things do not go their way. The fact of the blessing, and the way of the blessing, establish the dialectical relationship between God and the people as a permanent two-way street.

SIDRAH VA-YEZE
Double Standards of Morality

The picture we have of our forefathers is probably one of great sages bent over in prayer and study with much intellectual, but hardly any physical, muscle. This image, however, is contradicted by the facts. The heroic efforts of Avraham are well known. Less well known are the exploits of Yaakov. Yaakov, we are told, is so buoyed at seeing Raḥel that he is able to roll off the heavy stone covering the well, so that the flock of Lavan can be fed. He was able to do this even though the shepherds gathered around had told him that only a combined effort of all the shepherds pushing together could roll off the stone (Bereshit 29:3, 8, 10).

It is well known that human beings, when faced with emergencies, may on occasion do things that boggle their own imaginations. A person of average strength seeing a person trapped underneath a car might single-handedly move the car to free the trapped person. Later on, that person may not believe what actually occurred.

This type of instant strength is an indication that often the dropping of preconceived inhibitions about certain physical accomplishments actually makes those accomplishments possible. It speaks about the individual's human capacities, as much as it speaks of that individual's physical prowess. It is therefore still not clear whether Yaakov was physically strong. The answer comes a little later on.

Having been repeatedly cheated by his father-in-law, Yaakov and his family decide to leave after twenty years of service. They sneak away, fully aware that Lavan will not agree to their leaving. Lavan chases after them. He rebukes Yaakov for stealing away and even tells him that "it is in the power of my hand to do you harm" (Bereshit 31:29). Lavan goes on to say that God appeared to him in a dream and told him to behave, to refrain from attacking Yaakov. No doubt this remark irked Yaakov. Did Lavan think that he was a weakling who could not take care of himself? Was he threatening him in order to force him into a one-sided agreement?

Later on, after much heated dialogue, Lavan and Yaakov come to an agreement. They agree to a mutual pact of noninterference and nontrespass. The pact is struck around a rock.

"Yaakov took a stone and set it up for a pillar" (Bereshit 31:45). The word, *vay'rime'hah* (and set it up) is peculiar, for just a bit earlier, when Yaakov set up a pillar, the word used is *vayasem* (he placed). There is here the suggestion that the word *vay'rime'hah* means that Yaakov literally picked up the heavy pillar as if it were a small ball. This was his response. Imagine the menacing gesture this must have seemed to Lavan, seeing the "weakling" Yaakov lifting a heavy pillar. Yaakov was responding to Lavan's assumption that he had the power to do him harm, by showing him that he was no slouch.

Nevertheless, in spite of all this, the deal that is struck between Lavan and Yaakov turns out to be one-sided. The Gaon of Vilna points out that there were two objects used for the treaty —the *mazayvah* (the monument; alternately referred to as *mizpah*) and the *gal*, the heap. The Gaon suggests that *gal* relates to *megulah*, meaning "obvious," whereas *mizpah* relates to *zafun*, meaning "hidden." Lavan was only obligated to avoid obvious trespass, his was a *gal* treaty. But, as far as Yaakov was concerned, even hidden trespass was forbidden; Yaakov's was a *mizpah* treaty. Thus, Lavan says that "if you afflict my daughters and if you take wives besides my daughters" (Bereshit 31:50), it will be a breach of their agreement.

In effect, Yaakov had to be moral not only to the outside world, but even within his four walls, in his thoughts and actions. Yaakov had accepted this for himself long before signing the agreement with Lavan. The double standard of morality here imposed by Lavan is only a prototype of what has happened throughout history. Many nations have demanded a form of moral superiority from the Jew. This has given them carte blanche to attack the Jew at every turn for not being as morally superior as they were supposed to be.

Yaakov accepted Lavan's terms, but not in Lavan's context. He accepted the responsibilities of a higher morality, not out of weakness, but out of strength; not because it was imposed, but because it was presupposed. By his show of strength, he categorically rejected the right of anyone to impose a double standard of morality.

The message of this dialogue between Yaakov and Lavan remains clear in our time. Note, for example, the illegitimate accusations hurled against the Jews, accusations which are not only untrue but also indicative of a double standard. Arab states are allowed to persecute Jews with impunity, but Israel is held culpable by those who consider even thriving business people in the "administered territories" to be "refugees."

In this age of double standards, Yaakov's approach stands out. The Jew accepts a higher standard of morality not for the sake of being superior and not because of being the weaker, but out of the strength and conviction that this is the way to live.

SIDRAH VA-YISHLAḤ
Prayer Perspective

How do you prepare for a confrontation with your brother, a confrontation which may be brotherly or may be explosive? The best general advice is to cover all eventualities, to be prepared for anything. It is the strategy of hoping for the best and preparing for the worst.

Rashi indicates that Yaakov, in anticipation of meeting head-on with Esau and his army of 400 people, prepared himself in three ways—with gifts, with prayer, and with war strategy (Bereshit 32:9). Obviously, from the fact that war strategy is mentioned last, we can assume that this was the least desired alternative. Yaakov knew that in a war, the most he could hope for was that part of his entourage escapes. Yaakov prepared for the worst, for a strategy for escape, a strategy which he hoped would never be necessary. The first item on his strategy list, gifts, would seem to fit into the "hoping for the best" component of the preparations. Yaakov was prepared to set a positive mood in this meeting, by offering significant presents to Esau. He hoped that this show of largesse, this display of humility and friendliness, would create a peaceful and tranquil mood, and thus forestall any military conflict.

It is the second part of the strategic preparations that is slightly problematic—prayer. If this is intended as prayer to God, then this should have been the first component of the strategy. Why is it only the second component of the overall plan?

There are two possible ways to approach this question. One is to suggest that Yaakov realized that as much as he was dependent on God's help, he could not legitimately pray to God for help without demonstrating that he was taking initiatives of his own. It is one thing to realize that you need God on your side; it is another to one-sidedly rely on God. By so doing, you do not show faith, you show a certain amount of arrogance, thrusting a challenge at God by putting all the responsibility in God's lap.

Yaakov could only be comfortable with asking for God's help after having mulled over what he should do and having carefully weighed the logic of his decision. Thus, it is likely that his prayer to God may have been to ask for God's help that he might carry the day by giving the gifts, enlisting God's help by instilling peaceful and loving thoughts in the mind of Esau.

There is another possibility: prayer to God was not at all part of the strategy with regard to Esau. Prayer was a vital component of Yaakov's life and was undoubtedly expressed in the anxious moments prior to the great confrontation. But that prayer to God had nothing to do with Yaakov's strategy regarding Esau. The prayer referred to here is quite possibly the prayer that Yaakov planned to invoke in his approach to Esau. If the gift giving did not work, then Yaakov was literally prepared to get on his knees to beg Esau to spare his family. He would not allow this meeting to become a battle of egos, with intransigence on both sides leading to tragic consequences. Instead Yaakov, to protect his family, was willing and ready to swallow his pride, to pray to Esau, to exercise emotional restraint in order to allow the family to continue on its way.

However we understand the connotation of prayer in Yaakov's plans, the implications for perspective on prayer are quite revealing.

SIDRAH VA-YESHEV
Rising to the Challenge

The notion that what happened to the Patriarchs is a harbinger of what is to occur to their descendants is perhaps most eloquently projected in the interaction between Yosef and his brothers. Yosef shares with his brothers his dream of domination over them, which arouses their envy. When he goes out to report on their activities, they conspire to kill him, with the attendant thought that "we will then see what will be of his dreams" (Bereshit 37:20). Obviously, if they kill Yosef, he will then be unable to dominate them. In the end, they do not kill Yosef. They get rid of him by selling him as a slave.

Who utters the thought "we will then see what will be of his dreams"? Ostensibly it is the brothers. But Rashi indicates otherwise, that this is spoken by a holy spirit. The holy spirit (*ru'aḥ haKodesh*) asserts that we will then see what will be of his dreams, as if to say to the brothers. "You may plot all you want, but if the dreams are destined to be, nothing will stop them from unfolding."

The comment of Ktav Sofer is quite illuminating. He suggests that the brothers, in wanting to kill Yosef, sank to a moral abyss. They may have been wronged by Yosef, and had some justification for their anger. But the minute they thought in terms of murder, they forfeited any claim of righteousness in the conflict.

Yosef, on the other hand, began this episode at the bottom, speaking and acting foolishly. In confronting death at such a young age, he was forced to mature quickly. He probably realized the folly of his ways and that vanity was of no value in leading a meaningful life. In that moment of crisis, with his life in the balance in a dangerous pit, he had a spiritual awakening which catapulted him into a spiritual sphere that he likely would not have reached so early in life.

The heavenly voice is thus the voice of eminent reason. It is the voice which says that those who are oppressed gain a strength and resolve through that oppression, which enables them to transcend any previous fault. On the other hand, oppressors, however they may justify their actions, become victimized by their cruelty and sink to base behavior.

This turns out to be a painfully accurate paradigm of Israel's history. Others strove to destroy Israel, but Israel just wanted to live. Whatever dreams it may have had, many nations contrived to deny Israel these dreams. However cultured, however advanced these nations may have been, in their attempts to stifle the Jews they sank to the bottom.

Israel, on the other hand, fighting as it did to survive, gained a better perspective on life. Instead of focusing on pleasure and thrills, it was involved in a life-and-death struggle for survival and meaningful living. In this process, it ennobled itself and future generations.

To this day, the holy spirit says to those who would stifle Israel's dreams: "We will see what will be of those dreams."

SIDRAH MI-KEZ
Folly of Hate

It was Jean Paul Sartre who once said that the anti-Semite, if he did not have any Jews available to hate, would invent them. This seems to be the case with the Egypt of biblical times. It is reported that they considered it an abomination to eat bread with the Hebrews (Bereshit 43:32). What Hebrews lived in Egypt at that time that made eating bread with them an abomination? There were no Hebrews in Egypt at that time, since the family of Avraham had not yet descended into Egypt. Yosef was a Hebrew who lived in Egypt, but the Egyptians were as yet unaware that he was a Hebrew.

The Targum indicates that the abomination inhered in that the Hebrews ate what Egyptians venerated as their God, namely the sheep. Their refusal to eat bread with the Hebrews was symbolic of their refusal to eat a meal with the Hebrews, a meal in which the Hebrews might actually eat the venerated sheep. The Egyptians would then painfully watch the indignity heaped upon their theology.

In the end, Yosef saved Egypt from the ravages of famine through his dream interpretation. Dream interpretation revealed to Yosef the strategy necessary to save Egypt: storing the grain for the forthcoming years of famine. Yosef's meteoric rise could have been achieved through some other means; for example, he could have been in the right place at the right time to save Pharaoh from a wild horse. The fact that this miraculous redemption came through grain exposes the folly of hate, the folly of anti-Semitism. The Egyptians refused to eat bread with the Hebrews. But it was only through the help of a Hebrew that the Egyptians were able to eat bread at all.

It is silly to hate, and self-defeating to create artificial barriers. Rather than cast aside and isolate the Hebrews, as they originally did, Egypt learned to its great relief and advantage that the Hebrews, given the opportunity, can provide wisdom and ample contribution to the betterment of society. The hatred directed at the Jew, at anyone for that matter, is ultimately a hatred that backfires on the perpetrator of that hatred. By loving and welcoming the Hebrew, the Israelite, the Jew, or any other distinctive group, society is much more likely to be enhanced. Hate deprives what love provides.

The very last words of the book of Bereshit report that Yosef died, and that he was embalmed and placed in a coffin in Egypt (Bereshit 50:2b). Normally, the conclusion of a reading is on an upbeat note. It seems a little odd that we should end an entire *sefer*, an entire book, with Yosef's death and his being placed in a vault!

However, the fact that the Egyptians placed Yosef in a vault indicates that they venerated him, and wanted to treasure his memory by putting him in a place where he would be preserved. As much as this may be antithetical to Judaic tradition, it is a laudable reaction, in that it shows profound appreciation. It also shows that the Egyptians, at least at that moment, overcame some of the animosity they harbored toward the Hebrews. This is thus an upbeat rather than a negative way to end the *sefer*.

Unfortunately the next *sefer*, Shemot, begins with some unpleasant developments concerning Israel's stay in Egypt. But for the moment at least, the Torah savors Egypt's having surmounted some of its undesirable tendencies.

SIDRAH VA-YIGGASH
The Transcendent Ingredient in Parenthood

There are few epic stories that equal the fall and rise of Yosef for sheer drama and emotion. One of the many climactic moments in the story, and no doubt the grand finale, was Yosef running to meet his dear father Yaakov, who earlier mourned the loss of his son and was beyond being comforted (Bereshit 37:35).

According to the Torah (Bereshit 46:29), Yosef fell on his father's neck and wept for a long time. There is no report of the emotional reactions of Yaakov. Ramban assumes that these words about falling on the neck and weeping refer not to Yosef, but to Yaakov. It was Yaakov who did the crying, as would be natural under the circumstances. Rashi, however, alluding to a statement of the Rabbis, asserts that indeed Yaakov did not fall on Yosef's neck and did not cry. Why? Because he was occupied with reciting the Shema.

At first glance, this seems to be a terrible anticlimax. Yaakov is about to meet his long-lost son. Instead of being overcome with joy and embracing his son, as would be the natural paternal inclination, he recites the Shema. Surely, he could have recited the Shema earlier.

The best way to approach this perplexity is through understanding the meaning of fatherhood and the significance of the Shema. Shema expresses the monotheistic ideal of the unity of God. It affirms faith and establishes the dominion of God over the world. It is a commitment expressed in word and in deed, to affirm godliness in one's personal life and in the life of the community, beginning with one's children.

What is fatherhood? Fatherhood emanates from a responsibility to propagate. But fatherhood is not merely a physical act; it is a spiritual obligation, an obligation to endow posterity with a sense of meaningfulness, value, and commitment that spring from a God-centered lifestyle.

Fatherhood is not expressed in relating to a child as a buddy, in satisfying the child's needs, or in making sure not to lose the child. It is expressed by inculcating in the child a sense of awareness that will motivate the child to grow, to mature. The successful Jewish father is one who has been able to instill in his child a sense of commitment that is strong enough to weather all storms.

It is difficult to project what went through Yaakov's mind as he was about to meet his long-lost son, but he undoubtedly worried about whether the educational foundation he had given Yosef was strong enough to enable Yosef to remain true to his commitments. This was of transcending importance to Yaakov. Yaakov's question was: could he say the Shema? Could he affirm that the tradition of faith has been carried on by Yosef? If he could, then it would mean he had not lost his son—neither physically nor spiritually.

When Yaakov and Yosef met, Yosef fell on his father and kissed him. Yaakov said the Shema. This was the spiritual kiss which made the physical presence a spiritual experience. Just from looking at Yosef, he could sense that the continuity he was so worried about was being perpetuated. In this profound reaction, Yaakov expressed what it means to be a Jewish father.

SIDRAH VA-YEḤI
Equal but Fair

Yaakov, as he prepares to leave his family, to depart from the world, blesses all his children. But before he blesses the children, he addresses the unique situation of Yosef and his children, born in Egypt. He blesses the grandchildren, and also tells Yosef that he has given to him an extra portion, more than all the other brothers (Bereshit 48:22).

A little while earlier, when Yosef meets his beloved brother Binyamin, he gives him five changes of clothing, fivefold more than he had given to the other brothers (Bereshit 45:22). In reaction to this, many commentaries wonder how Yosef, who had been the victim of special treatment and the envy that it aroused, could do the same thing with his brother.

However, when Yaakov announces to Yosef that he has given him an extra portion, there is barely a murmur from the commentaries. Yaakov, who had already suffered through twenty-two years of thinking that his son was dead, because of an ugly set of circumstances generated by the brothers' envy of Yosef, here seems to repeat his nearly fatal mistake of the past. His singling out of Yosef precipitated the ill will which degenerated into the brothers' intense hatred for Yosef.

Why did Yaakov here single out Yosef and seemingly repeat the error of the past? Previously it was with a coat, now it was with a piece of land. Nevertheless, it was still a significant singling out of one brother over the others. Rashi comments that the extra portion given to Yosef was Yaakov's way of showing his appreciation to Yosef for undertaking to take care of Yaakov's burial (Bereshit 48:22).

The fact that Yosef assumed this responsibility is in itself noteworthy. One may conjecture that Yosef was uniquely positioned to promise this, since he was of such high rank in Egypt and probably had free reign to do almost as he pleased. On the other hand, a high-ranking Egyptian dignitary wishing to take his father out of Egypt faced a unique set of problems. This unfolded later on, when Yosef had to convince Pharaoh to grant him permission to bring Yaakov to Hevron for burial (Bereshit 50:4-6).

Additionally, the other brothers were certainly not as busy as Yosef. Any one of them could have easily undertaken to assure the father that he would be buried with his family. In spite of this glaring disparity of time availability, it is Yosef who assumes responsibility for burial.

All this suggests that after Yaakov came to Egypt, Yosef resumed the closeness that he had with his father in his earlier years, although this time on an obviously more mature level. It seems as if time and distance did nothing to compromise the intense love between Yaakov and Yosef. Surely there was a love relationship with all the children, but it was Yosef who went the extra mile. It is likewise probably true that the other brothers understood the specialness of the relationship—that Yosef was always the one to go out of his way for their father.

Thus, when it came time for Yaakov to prepare for his demise, he singles out Yosef. But this time, the singling out of Yosef is more than deserved. It is the quid pro quo of a parent making a very simple statement. This statement is that even though it is not right to single out one child from many, if one child stands out above the rest in devotion and dedication, then there is nothing wrong with a parent showing appreciation to that child.

It is right to have equality within the family, but it is not right for children to demand that equality when they do not behave in a way that is deserving of such equal treatment.

Yaakov's original favoring of Yosef was unfair and unwise. The later singling out of Yosef by Yaakov was a fair, wise, and telling statement about the dialectical relationship between parent and child.

SIDRAH SHEMOT
Justifiable Skepticism

The agonizing story of Israel's servitude in Egypt is paralleled by the painful attempts of Mosheh Rabbenu to convince the Israelites that he is their leader and that he will be God's agent in redeeming them from their bondage. God gives Mosheh Rabbenu the appropriate signs by which he will establish his credibility with the people. After expressing great reluctance, Mosheh Rabbenu finally does meet the people and, together with Aharon, convinces them that redemption is near.

Mosheh and Aharon then implore Pharaoh to let Israel go. Pharaoh not only refuses, he also exacerbates an already oppressive burden. He maintains the same production quota but now refuses to supply the straw to make the bricks. The people of Israel are angered at Mosheh and Aharon and complain bitterly about their worsened lot. As far as they are concerned, Mosheh and Aharon have not improved things. They prefer that Mosheh and Aharon leave matters alone, rather than attempt to improve them and, in the process, make them worse (Shemot 5:1-21).

There is hardly a murmur in the commentaries about the behavior of the people toward Mosheh and Aharon. They are not rebuked for their lack of faith, they are not castigated for their impatience, they are not criticized for their bitterness.

The silence in this regard is deafening. The silence itself is also an eloquent expression of sympathy with Israel. The people's reaction in confronting Mosheh and Aharon is more than merely beyond criticism; it is praiseworthy. They felt that anyone who claims to be a redeemer must prove the claim via tangible results. Any claim to salvation that is not justified by subsequent results cannot be given credence.

In other words, anyone making messianic claims on the community receives no carte blanche. A messiah, a prophet, or any leader, must deliver on promises, or else the claim to prophecy or leadership is an obvious fraud.

Had this instantaneous and spontaneous reaction of Israel been employed in later periods of Israel's history, when many fraudulent leaders appeared on the scene, we would have avoided many false messiahs and the subsequent disasters they brought upon the Jewish people.

The reason there is no criticism of Israel's complaints to Mosheh and Aharon is that the complaints were legitimate, proper, well-placed, and deserved. It is only unfortunate that future generations did not react in the same way.

SIDRAH VA-ERA
Vigor of Old Age

Only once does the Torah report on the age of Mosheh at a specific point in his life and in the life of Israel. This is when Mosheh and Aharon come together to confront Pharaoh. Mosheh is reported to be eighty years old, and Aharon, eighty-three (Shemot 7:7).

Why does the Torah mention the age of Mosheh and Aharon specifically here? Perhaps it is to suggest that this is a tribute to them, in that they undertook a difficult mission at this later stage in their lives.

Eighty is deemed to be the age of strength (Mishnah Avot 5:24), but to us this idea hardly seems plausible. We firmly believe that people are usually stronger in their thirties or forties. Surely Mosheh and Aharon exhibited strength when they were in their eighties, but to say that the eighties are the years for strength seems to stretch the point.

This is the case, unless we understand the idea of strength in a different context. Obviously bodily vigor, pure muscular strength, is greater at the age of forty. But strength of will, vigor of purpose, obstinacy and uncompromising resoluteness may only come at the later age, after one has seen the vagaries of life and has a better appreciation of what is essential and what is trivial.

By the time one reaches the age of eighty, one is better able to sift out priorities. If blessed with energy, one exhibits the strength of uncompromising purpose in pursuing whatever needs to be pursued. At that time one is too old to be blandished by material rewards and usually too wise to be duped by rationalizations. In one's eighties, one has very little to lose and everything to gain. Ultimately, this gain is on behalf of posterity.

It is perhaps this that is highlighted in the Torah's report of how old Mosheh and Aharon were when they confronted Pharaoh. Their age is a significant factor in the credibility of the mission. They are not impetuous youths coming to start a fight. Nor are they arguing for personal betterment or political gain. They are beyond that stage. Whatever they ask for is thus obviously well thought out, and is not for themselves but on behalf of their people.

This sets up an interesting paradigm of communal leadership. It is true that Jewish leaders have always tended to give special attention to the youth, who are the foundation and backbone of the community's future. However, it is also recognized that true leadership in its ultimate sense comes from individuals more advanced in years. Such leadership is more likely to be beyond ego fulfillment. Instead, it is more likely to be an expression, in vigor, of the age-old commitment to Jewish destiny.

SIDRAH BO
A Matter of Principle

At various stages in the ongoing diplomatic wars that were waged by Mosheh against Pharaoh, demands were made and either rejected or met with unacceptable offers. The original demand of Mosheh that Pharaoh let the people go is spurned. Later, at various times, Pharaoh agrees to let the people go, as Mosheh demanded on behalf of the people, only to retract his agreement at the last moment.

At one point Pharaoh agreed to let the older members go but required that the younger ones stay; this offer was rejected (Shemot 10:9-11). At a crucial point, Pharaoh offered to let the entire community go, the old and the young. His only condition was that the sheep and the cattle remain (Shemot 10:24). Of course, there was no guarantee that having made the offer, Pharaoh would not once again retract it.

But Mosheh Rabbenu did not give him the chance; he declined the offer. Not only did he refuse the condition, he added a condition of his own. He said that not only would the people leave with their own sheep and cattle, but that Pharaoh would provide them with more of the same so that they would be able to offer sacrifices to God (Shemot 10:25-26). Why did Mosheh Rabbenu reject Pharaoh's offer? Why did he then place greater demands on Pharaoh?

It is possible, although there is no proof for this conjecture, that if Pharaoh had let the people go when Mosheh and Aharon made their original request, Mosheh and Aharon would have left the sheep and cattle behind if that was the only outstanding point of negotiation. It was only when the confrontation took on an added dimension that the matter of the sheep and cattle became important. At first, the critical matter was the enslavement of the people of Israel and the need to extricate them from this enslavement. Had Pharaoh agreed immediately, he would have signaled that the enslavement was a grievous error and that it was appropriate to rectify this error.

However, Pharaoh did not recognize the error. Instead he was intransigent and arrogantly maintained the murderously cruel policy. Pharaoh set himself up as more powerful than God and rejected God. With this, he escalated the battle from a human rights issue to a matter of ideological and theological principle.

Mosheh Rabbenu, sensing that the end was in sight, that it was only a matter of time before Israel would leave, was no longer willing to settle for simple release. He wanted Pharaoh to acknowledge his crime, the human rights abuse, and the theological outrage of arrogating to himself Divine right. There is a twofold reason for this desire of Mosheh.

First, there is too much of a connection between Pharaoh's idolatry and his insensitivity to human suffering. Second, there is the fear that over the course of the years in Egypt, some of the paganistic ideas held by the Pharaohs may have seeped into the Israelite subconscious.

Mosheh Rabbenu therefore insisted that before the Israelites leave, Pharaoh must admit that he was wrong. He must acknowledge that God rules over all and that paganism is a bankrupt theology. Mosheh Rabbenu wanted Pharaoh's clear statement to the world that he was wrong, that what was done to Israel was morally wrong and theologically inexcusable. This would hopefully discourage any nations that may have contemplated emulating Pharaoh's policies.

Mosheh Rabbenu also wanted Israel to hear that message, so that they might realize the folly of paganism. The most effective way for the message to be conveyed was for Pharaoh to provide the sheep and cattle that would be used to acknowledge God. Pharaoh would thereby admit, in a very public way, that he was wrong and that the way of Israel is the eminently correct way.

SIDRAH BE-SHALLAḤ
Eternal War

The unprovoked and unwarranted attack of Amalek on Israel is perceived, for perpetuity, as not merely an attack on Israel. This is a war of God with Amalek (Shemot 17:16). If this is the case, it can only be so if Amalek's original attack was not only against Israel but also against God. How is this reflected in the actual events?

The Torah begins the episode of Amalek with the simple words "Then Amalek came" (17:8). Ktav V'Kabbalah states that these words indicate that Amalek broke the normal protocols of war. Normally, the attacking army sends an emissary to announce the war. Amalek refused to do this. It *came* and warred, instead of first sending an emissary and then attacking.

The attack was launched in a place called Refidim. Although there is one view that the name "Refidim" is a play on words suggesting that Israel weakened its hand from the Torah (*rafu yedayhem*), the view of Rabbi Eliezer (Sanhedrin 106a) is that "Refidim" is simply the name of the city. In the words of Midrash Tanḥuma, Refidim is "as it suggests" (i.e., a city).

But what does Refidim suggest? Refidim was the last stop of Israel before they were to receive the Torah. One can assume that the giving of the Torah on Mount Sinai, just after the Refidim stop, was an open secret. Since the Torah was offered to the other nations, they obviously would have known that it was about to be given.

Amalek came at Refidim, but not because it had any territorial conflict with Israel. Its conflict was with God. Amalek simply did not want God to have a people. But since one cannot wage war against God directly, the only option left is to make war against those people who have affirmed their allegiance to God. By killing all those who have sworn allegiance to God, it is possible to maintain a godless society, wherein despots rule as self-appointed gods. Whereas other nations merely refused to accept the Torah, Amalek sought to assure that no one would accept the Torah, that higher morals and ethics would not be viable categories of human discourse.

It is for this reason that God declares that the war Amalek launched against God will be met with commensurate reaction. Even though it is a war against God, it is not as if the people are not involved. This war against Amalek is a battle against the vilifying forces seeking to delegitimize Israel, either by killing Israel off, or by making Israel into a pariah among the nations. The Amalek types will stop at nothing to detach God from Israel, Israel from God, and both God and Israel from civilization. It is a battle Amalek cannot be allowed to win.

SIDRAH YITRO
Humble Deservedness

The dominant theme of Sedra Yitro is the giving of the Torah. Concerning this, there is a fascinating episode reported in the Talmud (Shabbat 88b-89a). The angels are reported to have challenged God's giving of the Torah to mortals. They felt that since this was a godly document, it should remain in the heavens, where the godly reside, rather than be given to humans, who are obviously tainted.

God then instructs Mosheh Rabbenu to respond to the angels. Mosheh Rabbenu takes up the challenge. The gist of his answer is as follows: Do you work, that you need to cease on the Shabbat? Do you have any tendency to evil among you, that you need legislation forbidding adultery? Do you have envy among you, that you must legislate the prohibition of stealing? We humans have all these deficiencies, and therefore we need the code. The angels acknowledged the validity of Mosheh Rabbenu's argument, and the case was closed.

Why does God ask Mosheh Rabbenu to answer? If God wanted to give the Torah to the world, God should have simply told the angels not to interfere. It may be that it was important for God to understand why Mosheh was accepting the Torah on behalf of the people. It was likewise important for Mosheh to understand why he was accepting the Torah on their behalf.

Mosheh Rabbenu could have been triumphalistic. He could have argued that the angels did nothing to deserve the Torah, whereas we, the people of Israel, endured so many years of servitude and suffered so much that we deserve it.

Had Mosheh Rabbenu resorted to that argument, it would have created serious problems, since such a triumphalistic attitude is a basic corruption of Torah. Mosheh Rabbenu understood that you do not receive the Torah because you are superior. Hopefully, through adhering to the Torah, your way of existence will become superior. But the basic reason for receiving the Torah is to discipline the individual and the community, to check desires and drives, and to channel them in the proper direction. The Torah must be accepted in humility, with acknowledgment that it addresses human deficiency; it is not indicative of human superiority.

SIDRAH MISHPATIM
Her Time

At the outset of Mishpatim, the laws concerning those who are designated as "slaves," but who are really "personal services employees," are delineated. Any doubt about whether these individuals are slaves is removed by the famous talmudic statement that whoever acquires a servant actually acquires a master (Kiddushin 20a). The rules in such relations are painstaking, with overwhelming responsibility placed upon the "master," who must never be disrespectful to the servant. If there is only one pillow, the "employee" uses it. Some slave!

The rule of the menservants is followed by the seemingly incongruous case in which a father sells his daughter to be a maidservant. What father would do this? The Talmud reveals that this case concerns one who sells his daughter because of desperate economic circumstances (Kiddushin 20a). If the daughter remains with her father, there may not be sufficient food to ensure her survival. The responsibility for her welfare is therefore transferred to another person, one who has the means to feed her.

This other person can either marry her or arrange for his son to marry her. Thus, the legislation, which at first glance seems to be cruel, is actually a biblical permission given to a desperate father. He can save his daughter and need not feel guilty about doing so, since such permission is biblically mandated.

It is in this portion that the Torah introduces some basic legislation concerning the marital requirements of husband to wife. It is in the rules of the maidservant that it is revealed that if the husband fails to live up to his obligations in food, clothing, and conjugal visitation, the wife may exit from the marriage. She even has the right to demand exit from the marriage.

The Torah, as in other instances, introduces this legislation precisely in an instance when there is a greater likelihood that people will neglect the obligation. For this reason, legislation prohibiting the destruction of trees is introduced in the portion concerning war, since it is during war that one is least likely to care about the welfare of trees. Since servants are more vulnerable to mistreatment, it is in the section concerning them that marital protocol is presented.

The husband must provide food, clothes, and conjugal visitation. The biblical word for conjugal visitation is *onah*. The word itself yields some significant insight into the conjugal union between husband and wife. The word *onah* can mean, and should mean, "her time." It refers to the time that by biblical law belongs to the wife. This is the precious time of intimacy. By saying that this is the her time, the Torah makes a telling comment regarding conjugal union. It is not the husband's time, the husband's opportunity to seek out his thrills. It is her time, a time that the husband, by his warmth, understanding, and love, can make uniquely hers. That is his obligation.

On the other side of the coin, the word *onah* is also related to affliction (*eenui*). This is a commonly used word in biblical parlance (see Bereshit 31:59 and Va-yikra 23:27, 29:32). What should ideally be the woman's time, can unfortunately also be an affliction. This is the case if the husband, instead of desiring to please his wife, actually abuses her in his unbridled search for pleasure. This is a classic instance of marital rape; the wife is forced into conjugal union by a cruelly insensitive husband. Such conjugal visitation is never a fulfillment of the *onah* obligation; it is an affliction.

Thus, through the placement of the legislation, and in the word used to describe one of the key components of the marital compact, the Torah projects the idea that marital abuse, sexual abuse of the wife by the husband, is forbidden under all circumstances.

SIDRAH TERUMAH
Higher Religiosity

The Ark (*aron*) which housed the Ten Commandments was a fascinating structure. It was made of wood, with gold on the inside and the outside. The top covering of the Ark had two cherubic figures emanating from the gold. These figures faced each other (Shemot 25:20).

The Talmud poses an interesting question. In another place (Chronicles 3:13), it is reported that the cherubic figures pointed away from each other, toward the house (the walls of the Sanctuary). Why then, does the Bible state that the cherubic figures faced each other? The Talmud answers that the one is when Israel fulfills God's will, the other is when Israel does not adhere to God's will (Baba Batra 99a).

Ostensibly, the meaning of this response is that when Israel abides by God's will, the cherubic figures, young faces, look toward each other. However, when Israel does not abide by God's will, the cherubic figures do not face each other; they turn toward the wall. Is this a cause or an effect? Is the cherubic placement the cause of Israel' behavior, or is it the effect? Obviously the more logical assumption is that this is the effect, or the indicator, of Israel's behavior state.

This fascinating talmudic insight establishes a most vital guidepost for godly behavior. Godly behavior can be gauged from the way human beings interact with one another. If human beings behave toward each other in a respectful manner, in true dialogue, looking each other in the eye, facing one another, and trying to understand each other, then one can be assured that God is present in such a mode of communication.

However, if the human faces are turned away from each other, if they only care about themselves, and have turned their back on their fellows, then this is not merely a social slight. It is a theological blight. In a word, where there is *mentschlichkeit*, true human empathy and sensitivity, there is godliness. Where there is neglect of the other, then there is at the same time no true godliness. This, in the end, is the ultimate litmus test of true religiosity.

SIDRAH TEZAVVEH
Ordinary and Extraordinary

At the outset of Tezavveh, the *kohanim* are commanded, by the word of God transmitted to Mosheh, to light the *Ner Tamid*—the perpetual light—every day (Shemot 27:21). Immediately following this, Mosheh is asked by God to single out Aharon and his children to serve as *kohanim* (Shemot 28:1).

At first glance, the order seems to be inverted. It would have made more sense for the *kohanim*, Aharon and his progeny, to first be singled out for the task and then be told what they should be doing. Instead, they are told what they are to do before they are told who they are.

Why the reverse order? Interestingly, this reverse order is not unprecedented. Prior to Israel's accepting the entire code of law on Mount Sinai, they were given some commandments at Marah. Arguably, it was necessary for them to accept Torah that was more than just a mere abstraction. They needed some idea of what it was they were accepting. It is nice that they agreed to abide by God's word, but an inkling of what it was they were undertaking was necessary. Thus, they were given a little taste of what the obligations entailed.

The laws handed down at Marah all had one common denominator; they were regular, and, in most instances, daily components of life. In human interaction, the commandment given to them at Marah was related to the child's obligation to honor the parents. In regard to transcendent observances, they were told about the most regular of them—the Shabbat. With regard to other laws, they were told about the ones most likely to be part of the daily vocabulary, namely the social legislation that every community needs in order to function (Sanhedrin 56b).

This pattern was followed when Aharon and his sons were being chosen to serve as *kohanim*. They were first told about the most usual duty, the most regular and consistent of their obligations, namely, kindling the perpetual light. Once they had an idea and a taste of their obligations as *kohanim*, their being singled out had greater significance, since they were cognizant of the obligations for which they were selected, and still forged ahead.

There is a further message in the way that the *kohanim* were singled out. A *kohen* has a position of stature within the community. No one should expect to gain such a position simply by some Divine right. Stature is an achievement that is gained through work. It was only through their willingness to undertake the daily chores, the seemingly boring and onerous task of making sure that the perpetual light was kindled, that the *kohanim* could aspire to any stature within the community. If one is not willing to look after the ordinary, then one has no claim on the extraordinary.

SIDRAH KI TISSA
Unity for the Right Reasons

Sidrah Ki Tissa begins with the requirement that each individual contribute a half-shekel. Through this contribution, the proper count of the Israelite community would be ascertained.

The time for announcing the half-shekel obligation was traditionally set as the first day of Adar, the month in which we celebrate the festive day of Purim (Mishnah Shekalim 1:1). The Talmud (Megillah 13b) makes the following comment regarding the fact that the half-shekel obligation was announced on the first day of Adar: "It was known and clear to the One by Whose word the world came into existence, that Haman was destined to take out shekels against Israel. Therefore, God preceded their [Israel's] shekels to his [Haman's]."

But what is the message here? Is there anything gained from this mythical exercise of playing around with dates? What is the significance of orienting the annual announcement of the half-shekel around Haman's attempt to buy the right to destroy the Jews?

Haman's main argument to "justify" killing the Jews was that they were spread out in the kingdom and they were different, an unreliable, rebellious people whom it was worthless to maintain. There is strength in numbers, but less so when those numbers are spread out. With a weakened critical mass, any group becomes vulnerable. Certainly, infighting and bickering within a group likewise severely weakens the community's capacity.

The half-shekel contribution required of each individual was designed to impress upon the Israelites that they could only function as a community to their ultimate capacity, if they realized that each one alone is only half an entity and that they needed to combine with a counterpart to become a whole entity. The half-shekel conveyed the idea that each individual within the community was only a partial reality. To complete that reality, each individual had to link up to the community.

True enough, the community banded together when confronted with the serious threat to their existence posed by Haman. They were then united. But they were bound together for the wrong reasons. They were united not out of love for one another but out of fear of a common enemy. It is better to be united than separated, but it is infinitely better when the reason for unity is shared values rather than a shared fear of enemies.

Thus, the Talmud tells us that the half-shekel obligation was announced on the first day of Adar. This was to impress the community that it should be united not because of Haman's shekels but because of their half-shekels. The community should realize that adhering to the half-shekel philosophy is its most effective strategy in countering the designs of any Haman, no matter how many shekels or petrodollars are used to support diabolical designs for destruction.

SIDRAH VA-YAKHEL
Keeping Your Word, Your Thought

The people of Israel are gathered together by Mosheh Rabbenu, who urges all those who are genuinely concerned, to make generous contributions to the setting up of the *Mishkan* (Tabernacle). The Torah reports that Mosheh Rabbenu was eminently successful in this appeal, in that "All the willing-hearted brought . . ." (Shemot 35:22). They brought enough that they actually had more than they needed to establish the *Mishkan* (Shemot 36:7).

The willing-hearted are referred to in the Torah as *nediv lev*. Literally this means those who have donated in their heart. There is a vast difference between willing-hearted and those who donated in their heart. It may not be a difference in terms of the bottom line, but it is a difference in terms of the implications for philanthropy.

With regard to charity, it is stated, "That which comes out of your lips you shall observe and do . . ." (Devarim 23:24). From this we know that this is the case only if the commitment is uttered with one's lips. If it was only resolved in the heart, how do we know that such promise must be kept? For this it is written, "All the willing-hearted brought" (Talmud, Shavuot 26b).

This statement of the Talmud is codified in the Shulḥan Arukh (Yoreh Deah 258:13), where Rabbi Isserles in his gloss to the basic text states that if a person has resolved to make a donation to charity, even though that resolution has not been verbalized, it must nevertheless be carried out as if it had been verbalized. It is a sacred commitment, though it was only made in the heart.

This talmudic regulation gives us a profound insight into the previously cited Torah passage. All the willing-hearted brought—even those who were stirred by Mosheh Rabbenu's original impassioned appeal to help in the establishment of the *Mishkan*, and had decided in their minds what they were going to give, but had not verbalized their decision, gave according to that "heart" decision. Later, even though they may have had second thoughts, thinking that they had perhaps committed too much, or that it was not really that necessary, or that others were not giving as much as they were and that therefore they had an excuse for not giving. Nevertheless they kept to their original commitment, even though that commitment was only made in the heart.

With regard to charity, the obligation transcends simple social dynamics. It is more than merely being honest to a word that has been given to someone else. Charity is a sacred obligation. Reneging on a commitment in the heart is tantamount to turning one's back on God.

This heartfelt response to an appeal is of utmost moment. Rabbis and other communal leaders make many appeals; these are usually impassioned requests for worthy causes. Undoubtedly, many constituents are moved by these appeals and make some commitment in their hearts during the heat of the moment. However, when it comes to translating this into action, they find various and sundry excuses for lowering the amount, or perhaps not even giving at all.

When it comes to charity, the emotional giving in the heart is the reality that should carry the day. Charity is an emotional act. The person who later has second thoughts should reflect on which is the more authentic thought. Such a person may tend to dismiss the emotional commitment in the heart that arises during the heat of the appeal, saying, "I was carried away." This person may feel that the rational, sober analysis of the financial circumstances, and the subsequent diminished giving, are the more honest reflection of reality.

Jewish law says just the opposite. It is in the emotion of the moment that the true nature of a person's charitableness comes forth; it is that which should be carried out in practice. Hopefully, by making the commitment on the table equivalent to the commitment in the heart, people will realize that it is the heart that should be the guiding force in the sharing process.

SIDRAH PEKUDEI
Neatness Counts

After the instructions had been given concerning the specific garments that had to be worn by the *kohen* and the chief *kohen*, (*kohen gadol*), the Torah reports that all the instructions were followed.

One of the instructions is that the *ḥoshen* (breastplate) be tied to the ephod (an apron-like garment) and that the *ḥoshen* not move from the ephod, as God instructed Mosheh (Shemot 39:21). This is in compliance with a previous directive (Shemot 28:28) that the *ḥoshen* not move off the ephod.

The names of the tribes were imprinted on two of the unique garments of the *kohen gadol*. They were found on the two stones that were on the shoulders of the *ḥeshev ha'ephod* (connector to the ephod), six on each stone (Shemot 28:10, 39:7). Additionally, they were found on the *ḥoshen*, where each tribe had its name on one of the twelve stones (Shemot 28:21, 39:14).

The stones were placed on the *ḥoshen* in order that the tribes be remembered before God. But why was a second set of stones necessary? Possibly these stones, placed on the *kohen gadol*'s shoulders, would continually remind him that he carried the burden of all the tribes, that he had a sacred obligation to always be cognizant of this.

One may then suggest that the obligation that the *ḥoshen* not move from the ephod, that it be firmly fastened, is a symbolic message to the *kohen gadol*. He should never be loose or lax in the way he carries out his responsibility to the people. This is an obligation that should not give even an inch. It must maintain its unbending, tight, firm grip on the *kohen gadol*.

This suggestion is made with some trepidation, considering that *Sefer HaḤinukh* gives a different reasoning for why the *hoshen* is not permitted to move off the ephod. *Sefer HaḤinukh* states that if these were fastened in a loose manner, the *kohen gadol* would go about in a less than neat fashion. But the *kohen gadol*, as exemplar and model for the community, must always project a neat image. Whatever fits should fit exactly; it should not hang loosely. Symbolically, a loose fit gives the impression of not caring about how one appears. A careless appearance gives an impression of not caring in general. The *kohen gadol* was never allowed to do this.

Sefer HaḤinukh, perhaps sensing that this may not be the ultimate reason for the obligation, says that until we find a better reason for why the *hoshen* cannot move from the ephod, we will adhere to this one.

The previous reason is therefore suggested with some trepidation, and due deference to that great expositor of the meaning of the commandments. What is clear is that insofar as the Torah is concerned, neatness definitely does count.

SIDRAH VA-YIKRA
Divulging Painful Truths

Sidrah Va-yikra presents details of the various categories of offerings a person was obliged to bring in specific circumstances. There were obligatory offerings when an individual had erred or sinned. There were more optional offerings that a person could bring if the person so desired.

Among the potential breaches is the case in which an individual withholds testimony and then denies and lies concerning information that should have been forthcoming, claiming lack of knowledge about the matter. If the lie was exposed, a special atonement process was required.

This entire procedure relates to a primary obligation spelled out quite cogently by Rambam in his *Sefer HaMitzvot* (Mitzvah #178). There, Rambam states that we are commanded to testify before the *bet din* concerning anything we may know about a person, whether it be that through such testimony the person will become subject to the death penalty or will be saved or will lose money. We are obliged to testify in all this and to inform the judges of what we have seen or heard. This is a general, far-reaching, proactive obligation, the consequences of which are that if the person does not testify, that person shall bear the iniquity of withholding the testimony (Va-yikra 5:1).

The ramifications of this pervasive obligation are quite interesting. Western civilization is acclimatized to the adversarial system, whereby the state must build a case in order to convict an accused. Usually the accused is brought into the court as the outcome of a police investigation of an alleged crime and is then held over for trial, whenever that may be. There are individuals within the community who are charged with a specific responsibility to enforce the legal code, be they the police, or the state prosecutors, or the attorneys general.

The Torah system did not know of any prosecutor, hangman or any individual who had the responsibility to seek out criminals and bring them to justice. On the one hand, the Torah refused to place upon anyone the burden of having to be an enforcer, an individual who may become too powerful and too impressed with the authority and force that could be exerted. On the other hand, by not introducing the position of prosecutor, every individual in the community becomes a potential prosecutor. Any individual who knows of testimony that could remove a murderer from the scene or that could rectify a wrong that had been done to someone has no right to remain silent.

The best judicial system is one in which all citizens see themselves as responsible for everyone else and are ready, willing, and able to do what is obligatory in the specific circumstances—to protect and to correct. They need not be judge and jury, but they must be willing to come forward and share what they know, and then leave it to the court, the respected judges of the community, to decide on the merits of the case.

The idea that we are all responsible for everyone else includes the responsibility to divulge painful truths. But this is not done in a gossipy way. The truth is divulged only within the confines of a judicial system, in which the testimony shared can have a positive impact. We have no obligation to play detective, but we have no right to be neglectful when we have the opportunity to help others in need, even if that may be a judicial need.

SIDRAH ZAV
Thinking Big

The law of the *olah* offering forms the lead component of this Torah reading. In reference to the *olah*, the Torah mentions that it is consumed on its firewood (Va-yikra 6:2). The direct Hebrew translation for "its firewood" is *mokdah*. The first letter of that word, the *mem*, is smaller in size than the normal Torah lettering. Why? The *olah* is an offering that is brought to atone for having harbored wrongful thoughts. The *olah* offering that was to atone for these thoughts was brought in the daytime, but burned all through the night. It burned on *mokdah*, on its firewood, all night until the morning.

It has been pointed out that *zav*, the word used in commanding this sacrifice and by which this entire Torah reading is named, connotes zealousness and eagerness. The word *zav* literally means command. It is an order given to Aharon and his children concerning the *olah* offering. The command is intended to inspire greater action on the part of Aharon and his entourage in the bringing of the *olah* offering. The usual reason given for this extra emphasis on zealousness is that the *kohanim* do not gain as much materially from the *olah* offering, since it was entirely consumed on the altar.

But there may be another reason. The *olah* offering is for bad thoughts, not specific deeds. When there has been an overt commission of an obvious transgression, then the need for expiation through an offering is evident. However, if the offering is for thoughts alone, one may feel that the sacrifice is not as necessary. Hence the word *zav* is used in the command to emphasize to Aharon that he must be as eager and zealous with this as with all other offerings.

It is interesting to note that in the Hebrew word for thought, *mah'shavah*, the first Hebrew letter is a *mem*. Quite possibly, the small *mem* in the word *mokdah* refers to the thought processes themselves. The person bringing the *olah* offering is doing so because the thoughts were not big, noble, mature thoughts; they were small, immature, and perhaps even sinful thoughts.

Usually, such wrongful thoughts occur during the night. In the daytime, one is too preoccupied with daily concerns to have the time to think in deviant ways. Therefore, the *olah* offering is brought all through the night. It is suggestive of the idea that the individual who was consumed by small thinking should make amends for this, in a symbolic way, by consuming those thoughts rather than being consumed by them.

The burning fire that gets rid of this excess at the same time brightens the atmosphere and illuminates the surroundings. It is to be hoped that the person who has had these bad thoughts will see the message inherent in the procedure and move away from small thinking toward thinking big.

SIDRAH SHEMINI
When Kindness Isn't

Only certain animals are eligible to be kosher. To so qualify, the animal must be cloven-hoofed and rechew its food via a ruminating stomach. For fish to be kosher, they must have fins and scales.

However, concerning the fowl, there are no general rules. Instead, the Torah delineates all the fowl that are disqualified, that can never be eaten. The reason for this differentiation concerning the fowl is quite evident. With regard to the animal kingdom, an outward, obvious sign is adequate for identification purposes. However, with regard to the fowl, the disqualifying ingredient is not obvious. It is a behavioral factor rather than a biological one. As Ramban points out, the disqualifying characteristic of the fowl is cruelty (Va-yikra 11:8). In other words, the fowl that are not eligible to be kosher are all cruel fowl. But you will not always catch a cruel fowl exercising cruelty. It will therefore be difficult to positively identify the said bird as being unfit. Therefore, the Torah must list all fowl that are unfit.

Among the fowl that are so labeled is the *ḥasidah*, the stork. It is not immediately apparent what cruel property the *ḥasidah* possesses that should disqualify it. Rashi (Va-yikra 11:19) identifies the *ḥasidah* as the white stork. He mentions that it is called *ḥasidah* because it exercises *ḥesed* (kindness) with its friends concerning food sustenance.

Apparently, what is intended as an explanation to disqualify, seems at first glance to be an eminently laudable virtue. If it is the penchant of the *hasidah* to act kindly concerning food, why is it then disqualified?

A possible explication of this difficulty is found in a comment by Rashi on the Talmud (Hullin 63a), in which Rashi explains that the *hasidah* "doles out her food." In this doling out inheres the cruelty of the *hasidah*. Sharing with others in an unassuming, modest way is praiseworthy. However, doling out food in a way which makes the beneficiary feel embarrassed by the procedure is less an act of charity and more an act of insensitivity and arrogance.

The haves who make the have-nots grovel for their bread ruin their charity by the uncaring manner in which they distribute it. It is this quality of the stork's behavior that is its cruelty. To make others beholden to you and emotionally dependent upon you is not an act of benevolence. This is true for the stork and true for any other type of sharing. It is a "fowl" method, which is not kosher.

SIDRAH TAZRI'A
Why the Eighth Day?

It is a well-known fact of Jewish life that circumcision takes place when the child is eight days old. But why should the circumcision take place when the child is in its eighth day? Is there anything magical about the eighth day?

This question occupied the attention of the Sages of the Talmud (Niddah 31b). There the question is asked in blunt terms, Why did the Torah say that the circumcision should take place on the eighth day? The answer given is quite unexpected. In the words of the Talmud, it is so that the experience is not marked by the disparity between the happiness of all assembled for the circumcision and the unhappiness of the parents of the child.

Immediately, one wonders why the parents would be unhappy, when everyone else is happy. The unhappiness referred to here is something altogether removed from our normal parameters of thought. In the verse just prior to the one dealing with the time for the circumcision (Va-yikra 12:2), the Torah states that after childbirth, a woman must distance herself from her husband for seven days. On the eighth day the child is circumcised. But, by direct extension of the Torah's statement, the eighth day is also the day that husband and wife may resume physical contact. It is this unhappiness of separation that is the reason circumcision is delayed until the eighth day, the day husband and wife can fully embrace and share the joy of the moment.

From the aforementioned passage of the Talmud, we derive that it is important that the proper ambience for the observance of a commandment be generated. Since it is the parents who must raise the child and who are responsible for the child adhering to the covenant, it makes little sense that they be unhappy or distraught at the time of the circumcision. The circumcision is thus delayed in order that the parents be together, and happily together.

Midrash Rabbah (Devarim 6) asks the same question — Why do we wait until the eighth day? — and suggests a different approach. The answer in the Midrash is that we wait until the eighth day, so that the child is more functionally autonomous, and therefore better able to handle the trauma of circumcision and its aftereffects. The midrashic answer focuses on the child's general condition, rather than on whether the parents are together or not.

From the midrashic perspective it would seem as if the ideal time for circumcision would be immediately after the child is born, but the circumcision is delayed until the child is viable enough to tolerate the procedure.

But if circumcision is a covenantal act, why do we not delay the circumcision until the child is aware of the implications of the circumcision and is actually old enough to appreciate the full significance of the covenantal act? Why in fact do we not delay circumcision until the child is thirteen?

More importantly, why is this not even a question? It seems as if the framework of questioning is restricted to why we wait until the eighth day, why we do not circumcise even earlier than that. Why do we not even have some qualms about the circumcision taking place so early, rather than so late?

The simple answer to this is that there was never any contemplation of circumcision taking place as late as the age of thirteen. True, it is the time when the child can better appreciate the meaning of the covenant, but the pain involved is so excruciating as to make this advanced age off-limits as the time for circumcision. We would not want the child to associate entry into Jewish affirmation with excruciating pain. Therefore, the circumcision must take place at the earliest possible stage, when the pain is much less severe, and the child hopefully hardly aware of the pain.

Once the child has been circumcised, it becomes the obligation of the parents to assure that this is not merely a surgical procedure, but that the child appreciates the significance of the covenantal responsibilities placed upon it. To a large extent, the Bar Mitzvah at age thirteen is the child's reaffirmation, at the first moment of adulthood, of the agreement undertaken on his behalf when he was only eight days old. Bar Mitzvah is the painless but meaningful entry into the covenant, the process that was begun at the early stages of the child's life.

From the fact that the circumcision takes place on the eighth day, not earlier and not later, much is revealed about the essence of Jewish continuity. In a word, the eighth day is chosen because that is the day that the parents have come together again and are happy together. And it is a time when the covenantal affirmation is still relatively painless. The message is clear. Our children should grow up in an atmosphere of joy, wherein Jewish affirmation is looked upon not as a pain but as a pleasure.

SIDRAH MEZORA
Why the Hyssop?

In the procedure for the cleansing of the individual who was afflicted with *zara'at*—a type of skin plague—cedarwood, scarlet, and the hyssop were among the ingredients employed (Vayikra 14:4). Hyssop is also a component of the red heifer procedure (Be-midbar 19:6), as well as of the pascal sacrifice (Shemot 12:22).

Rambam, in the *Guide for the Perplexed*, openly admits that he does not know the reason for the hyssop—why it was used in the burning of the red heifer and why a bunch of hyssop was used for the sprinkling of the blood of the pascal lamb. Rambam humbly admits that he cannot find any reason to account for this species being singled out (*Guide for the Perplexed* III, 47).

It is dangerous, perhaps even presumptuous, to attempt explicating what Rambam could not explicate. What follows is a mere conjecture that may or may not hold true.

When God gave Mosheh the instructions for the pascal sacrifice, no mention was made by God of the bunch of hyssop. God merely states that the Israelites should take from the blood of the sheep and place it on the doorposts and the lintel (Shemot 12:7). The idea that the blood should be applied via a bunch of hyssop was given by Mosheh Rabbenu, apparently on his own, to the people.

The placing of the blood on the doorposts was an act of defiance by Israel, to show the Egyptians that they were not afraid. They would take the blood of the sheep (which was deified in Egypt) and blatantly tell Egypt that this was ridiculous idolatry. The Egyptians may have told the Israelites that it was *barbaric* to place blood on the doors. The Israelites would probably have countered that it was more barbaric to place babies into walls to make up the quota of bricks for structures.

However, whatever the dialectics of the sprinkling may have been, there was always a danger that in defiance the people would become arrogant. Mosheh Rabbenu was concerned with how to strike a balance. It was important for the people to show defiance, not solely for its own sake but also in order to establish firmly in the people's minds that they were now totally free from Egyptian bondage and idolatry, physically and emotionally. This can sometimes come at a very painful price, the price of becoming so self-assured that one is beyond any discipline. Possibly for this reason Mosheh asked the elders to dip the bunch of hyssop in the blood and then apply it. The hyssop, as the lowest plant, inspired humility. Mosheh Rabbenu hereby attempted to balance the act of defiance with the humbling procedure through which this act would be expressed.

The reentry procedure for the person who had become afflicted with *zara'at* and the red heifer procedure for the person who had come in contact with the body of one who has died both involved this hyssop.

Concerning the reentry procedure for the individual with *zara'at*, Rashi suggests that the cedar is symbolic of arrogance, which is the cause for the plague, and that it is counterbalanced by the thread of the worm (referred to as scarlet) and the hyssop, both of them lowly and humble species (Va-yikra 14:4). The message to the person on reentry is that humility is the order of the day and must be part of the reentry process.

However, this rationale for the hyssop does not readily apply to the situation in which the ashes of the red heifer are used. The contact with the body of an individual who had passed away is either a pure accident or a necessary circumstance (if the deceased was a relative, friend, or someone who had no other friends or relatives to arrange the burial). Why the hyssop in this instance?

The hyssop may here be slightly related to the hyssop that was first introduced by Mosheh Rabbenu in order to counterbalance an act of defiance and to assure a humble perspective. Possibly, and I emphasize possibly, the *tamay* individual who is now involved in reentry may feel a certain sense of satisfaction bordering on arrogance for having come back. After all, there is much attention given to the individual and there is a pronouncement that the individual is fit. All this special treatment cannot help but make an impression on the individual. The Torah, in introducing the hyssop in the reentry process, is perhaps gently telling the individual Yes, you are back, but do not become too enamored with yourself in the process. You are welcome, without any qualifications, but make sure that you do not become too impressed with yourself. If you are too impressed, then the reentry itself is on shaky foundation.

To a certain extent, this is a potent message to those in our generation who have made the very significant reentry into Judaism, those who have seen or were shown the light. In coming back, it is always best to come back with hyssop in hand, to be humble in the excitement and exuberance of having discovered the timeless traditions of Judaism.

SIDRAH AḤAREI MOT
Nothing New under the Sun

Western civilization is mired in a crisis concerning the matter of sexual morality. Supposedly new methods of sexual expression, such as homosexuality, are becoming more prevalent. Many who identify themselves as liberals have argued that these should be accepted as "alternate modes of sexual expression." Even within the religious sphere, there are some who argue that these modes of expression are consistent with the modern age and that religion, in order to be in tune with the times, should make accommodations for this.

However, it turns out that these so-called new modes are not new at all. Consider the biblical admonition "According to the ways of the land of Egypt you shall not do, and according to the ways of the land of Canaan to which I bring you, you shall not do, and their statutes you shall not follow" (Va-yikra 18:3). Sifra takes this as being a reference to homosexual behavior.

The Torah reference to the behavior of the Egyptians and the Canaanites indicates that this was more than just an unusual aberration or rare occurrence. It was normal and accepted. The Israelites were urged to reject this, even if ostensibly civilized societies engaged in such behavior.

What seems to be a new reality was in fact a norm long ago. It was a norm for purely self-serving reasons. Those individuals who wanted sexual thrills without attendant responsibilities, would opt for the homosexual relationship.

Homosexuality, at its very root, is a misogynistic behavior. In those societies, homosexuality was engaged in by people who used women merely as factories to produce children. For sexual thrills, they would go to the homosexual brothels.

The fact that the Torah exhorts the community of Israel to renounce homosexuality, even though it is a norm, and then proceeds to spell out the punitive implications for homosexuality (Va-yikra 20:13), clearly establishes that homosexuality in general is not an act of compulsion over which the human being has absolutely no control. If indeed homosexuality were of such a nature, there would be no justification for imposing a death penalty for the homosexual act. Human beings in general are exonerated from any act of compulsion over which they have no control (Talmud, Baba Kama 25b). The biblical exhortation clearly establishes that we do have control.

The admonition in the Torah against emulating the Egyptians and the Canaanites and following their statutes prompts Sifra to ask a simple question: Did not the Egyptians and the Canaanites engage in building and planting? Does this mean that the Israelites had to avoid building and planting because this was done by the Egyptians and the Canaanites?

Sifra rejects this possibility and points to the latter part of the passage, which states that "you shall not follow their statutes." What were their statutes? asks the Sifra. The statutes were that men marry men and women marry women. This is quite an illuminating observation of the Sifra. It suggests that the Torah made special mention and precise condemnation of legalizing the homosexual union through statute. Obviously, homosexuality was a prevailing practice, a practice probably engaged in by most nations. Egyptians and Canaanites were singled out not merely because these were the venues that Israel had been in or were going toward, but also because in these locales, homosexuality, be it of the gay or lesbian type, was legally entrenched. Going by the language of the Sifra, it was even forced upon the population.

The Torah therefore makes special mention of, and singles out for special condemnation, the legalization of homosexuality. The act in itself is roundly condemned as being an abomination. It is even worse when society takes that which is abominable and makes it legally acceptable. The prohibition, directed not only at the action but also at its legalization, although first postulated thousands of years ago, is obviously of great import in these turbulent times.

SIDRAH KEDOSHIM
As Yourself

The sixth of the seven blessings recited under the *huppah* expresses the wish that God will cause the beloved *re'im* to be as happy as God made Adam and Eve happy in the Garden of Eden. The question that arises is Why is the couple referred to by the term *re'im*? *Re'ah* means "neighbor," "friend"; why are they not called *haverim* ("friends") or *yedidim* ("beloved") or *zug* ("pair") or *shutafim* ("partners")? Why refer to them as *re'im*?

Furthermore, why refer to the happiness and bliss of Adam and Eve in the Garden of Eden? Is there any firm evidence that Adam and Eve were indeed so blissfully happy? Was their marriage any more ideal than that of Avraham and Sarah, or that of Yizhak and Rivkah, or that of Yaakov and Rahel? Why are they the paradigm for marital bliss?

One of the fundamental commandments within Judaism is the obligation to "love your neighbor as yourself. . . ." (Va-yikra 19:18). Ramban, among other commentators, reflects on the impossibility of actually living out this responsibility. It does not seem possible that an individual could ever love another person with the same intensity as one loves one's own self.

It is interesting that quite often in the Talmud this verse is used with specific reference to the marital relationship. Thus, the prohibition against marrying someone before seeing that individual is based on this verse. "Love your neighbor as yourself. . . ," and therefore make sure that you know your partner before you marry. In the words of the Talmud, with lack of knowledge, you may see something unseemly in the partner, and that may bring with it rejection, when in fact love should prevail (Talmud, Kiddushin 41a). The Talmud seems to assume that the most direct application of the obligation to love one's *re'ah* is within the marital sphere. The *re'ah*, the intimate friend, the spouse, one must love as one loves one's own self.

Loving someone who is an "other" is beyond possibility. Loving someone who is as your own self, as indeed is the case with one's spouse, is not only possible; it is also desirable.

In the Garden of Eden, Adam and Eve were originally one corpus but were later surgically separated (Talmud, Berakhot 61a). When we recite the blessing that the couple should be as happy as Adam and Eve, we are referring to the happiness of being as one; Adam and Eve were literally as one. The use of the term *re'ah* in the blessing, referring to the bride and groom as *re'im*, is to establish a direct connection with the terminology of *re'ah* in the obligation to love your neighbor (*re'ah*) as yourself.

Through loving your spouse as yourself, it is possible to reach that state of love which is based on the feeling of oneness, a reality which prevailed in the Garden of Eden and which, it is to be hoped, will likewise prevail within marriage.

SIDRAH EMOR
Why not a Divorcée

The people whom a *kohen*, or *kohen gadol* (chief *kohen*) are prohibited from marrying are listed at the outset of Sedra Emor. Among the various restrictions, the one that has greatest impact to this day is the prohibition forbidding an ordinary *kohen* from marrying a divorcée.

There are those who suggest that the prohibition indicates that there is a Judaic prejudice against divorcées. This is based on the assumption that the *kohen*, who occupies a more lofty position within the community, becomes somewhat "tainted" by marrying someone who had been previously married to another person.

This is the wrong conclusion. But what is the reason behind the prohibition, a reason which would lead to a different conclusion with regard to the status of a divorced woman?

The prohibition against marrying a divorcée may be traced back to an interesting process. In Temple times, a woman would go to the Temple to bring an offering following childbirth (Vayikra 12:6). This offering was to neutralize any negative thoughts that may have passed through the woman's mind during the birth process. Private offerings such as this, among other types of offerings, were preceded by a conversation with the *kohen* in order to assure that correct thought and intent accompanied the offering.

It may be assumed that immediately after childbirth, most women would be emotionally vulnerable, having just gone through what is at once an exhilarating and a traumatic experience. In the process of pouring out her heart to the *kohen*, it is possible that she may find the *kohen* to be much more understanding than her own husband. It is not out of bounds to fear that in such an emotionally vulnerable moment, the woman may begin to regret her choice of mate. She may harbor the desire to divorce her husband in order to marry the understanding *kohen*.

Had the change of husband occurred even just once or twice, the position of the *kohen* and his ability to serve the community would have been greatly compromised. He would have likely caused all husbands to think twice about letting their wives go to the *Bet HaMikdash* in the first place. This would have sabotaged a major conduit for legitimate religious expression.

Quite possibly in order to avoid such occurrences, the Torah prohibited the *kohen* from marrying a divorcée. This prohibition removed the worry about anything improper transpiring between the woman and the *kohen*, since any romantic links are automatically ruled out. This, among other reasons, may be the rationale for the prohibition. It makes no statement about a divorced woman being inferior at all.

In a larger sense, one can see the relationship of the *kohen* to the rest of the community as being theologically therapeutic. The biblical prohibition of marriage between a *kohen* and a divorcée may thus be interpreted as an attempt to maintain the integrity of the relationship of the *kohen* to the rest of the community. This prohibition, thousands of years old, thus offers advice on the therapeutic relationship which is quite contemporary and exceedingly apropos in its wisdom.

SIDRAH BE-HAR
Making Everything Count

The idea of counting is part of the Jewish vocabulary. In contemporary times, the count that stands out most is the one which links Pesaḥ to Shavuot. It is the Omer period of seven weeks, with the fiftieth day being Shavuot. This is a linkage count, connecting the notion of freedom to the idea of responsibility. It establishes that we became free on Pesaḥ in order to be able to live by God's word, the word revealed on Shavuot (Va-yikra 23:15-16).

There are other counts that form part of our lifestyle. They include the woman's counting of the days before going to the mikvah, certainly a more personal and private count. There is the more public count of each day leading up to Shabbat. This is the count that is recited at the conclusion of the daily prayers, through an appropriate psalm for that day, indicating in the prefix what day it is in the countdown to Shabbat.

With all the countings of which we are aware, there is a count that is of singular importance but which has disappeared from our counting patterns. This is the counting of seven times seven years, leading to the *yovel* year, the fiftieth year (Va-yikra 25:8). Torat Kohanim indicates that this count is not the responsibility of each individual. It is a responsibility which rests with the Great Sanhedrin, the Jewish High Court (*Bet Din HaGadol*).

According to Arukh HaShulḥan, the High Court would rise on Rosh HaShanah and recite a blessing which reads approximately as follows: "Blessed are you, Lord our God, Ruler of the universe, Who has sanctified us with the commandments and has commanded us concerning the counting of the *sh'mitah*. Today is the first year for the *sh'mitah*." On the eighth year, the count would be "Today is eight years, which is one whole sabbatical [seven years] and one year toward the jubilee [fiftieth year]." And so it would go on, much like the *berakhah* for the Omer that is counted to connect Pesaḥ to Shavuot.

Why is the count of the years delegated to the Great Sanhedrin, whereas the count of the days is given over to all Israel? Possibly because the count, linking Pesaḥ to Shavuot, is to impress each individual with the idea that their celebration of Pesaḥ should lead to a full acceptance of the Torah on Shavuot. It is not merely the community in general that is accepting the Torah. It is each and every individual within that community.

However, concerning the jubilee year, there are specific responsibilities on the fiftieth year that may not necessarily apply to every individual. Not everyone may have servants that need to be freed; not everyone may have land that must be returned; not everyone will have land for which there is a prohibition against planting and harvesting. It therefore becomes the obligation of the Great Sanhedrin to publicly do the counting. This reminds the people of what year in the cycle of the jubilee they are at present, and thereby enables them to prepare accordingly for the fiftieth year.

But there is more that is achieved through mandating that the Great Sanhedrin must publicly count the years leading up to *Yovel*. The counting creates a focus. At no point in the life of the community do they go from year to year in a disconnected, incoherent way. Instead, each year is connected to the next, and it all gears toward the climactic moment of the fiftieth year. That climactic moment is the time when everything returns to the original status quo. The land is left alone so that everyone has equal claim on it. The original division of the land is reestablished, and all individuals who are in servitude situations regain their freedom.

The high court reminds the entire community, through this public counting, that our lives should have a focus. That focus should always be directed toward expressing human dignity, and the responsibility to share with others. This is the purpose of the count. Through this we will make sure that every action and every person really counts.

SIDRAH BE-ḤUKKOTAI
Cause and Effect

A covenant is a two-way street. It involves an if-then relationship. If party number one will do so and so, then party number two will respond with such and such. That type of covenantal relationship is established at the very outset of Be-ḥukkotai. Israel is told, "If you walk in My statutes and keep My commandments and do them, *then* I will give your rains in their season and the land shall yield its produce, and the trees of the field shall yield their fruit . . . and you shall eat your bread to satisfaction and you will dwell in your land in tranquility" (Va-yikra 26:3-5).

At first glance, this seems to be a covenantal agreement. If the people will follow God's word, then they will be rewarded with bountiful yield, which they will enjoy in tranquility.

As welcome an arrangement as this may seem, it seems to be contrary to the basic principle that "There is no reward for the fulfillment of the precepts in this world" (Talmud, Kiddushin 31b). If the aforementioned covenant is taken as a reward, then it is a blatant contradiction of the idea that there is no reward for the fulfillment of the precepts in this world. The covenant states clearly that there is a reward, a very tangible reward at that, for the fulfillment of the precepts.

Concerning the promise that you will "eat your bread to satisfaction," Rashi, quoting Torat Kohanim, states that you will eat a little bit, but it will be blessed in your digestive system. This small observation may offer a hint as to the exact nature of what seems to be a covenantal affirmation.

The blessing is not one of bountiful yield. It is more a blessing of quality rather than of quantity. The little bit that you eat will be to satisfaction. It will not be necessary to have an abundance of food in order to feel satisfied.

There will be blessing, but it will be related to the people's mindset. They will not be on a gluttonous path. Instead, they will eat in a value-imbued way. Instead of consuming whatever they can, they will share with others and will be satisfied with the little bit that they do eat. This is the Torah concept of ideal consumption.

We are to be concerned not just with ourselves, but with the environment around us. We have no right to assume that the land is ours, and that we can therefore abuse it without thought as to the consequences of that abuse. We must be sure to give the land its rest on the sabbatical year. We must at the same time assure that the have-nots of the community are well taken care of through our bounty.

People who are outer-oriented, whose concern is for fulfilling values and transcending their selves, are much less likely to be narcissistic. Their needs are minimal, and they will be satisfied with little. They will thus have plenty to share with others less fortunate. This is what is included in this first part of the covenant, namely if you will follow my statutes and observe my precepts and do them. Actualizing this in its all-embracing implication inures to the ultimate of blessings, the blessing of a community which is fortunate to have caring citizens who look after the welfare of the populace.

What God is hereby introducing is not a reward for adherence to the precepts, as much as the spelling out of a cause and effect. The effect of individuals abiding by all the laws, laws to protect the ecology and the people within that ecological system, is that you will have tranquility. You will be able to enjoy whatever yield is forthcoming from the field and the trees. The tranquility will come from living in a society where the poor appreciate that the wealthy have not cut them off, but are deeply concerned about them. They will then not attack them, despoil them, or be envious of them. The trees in the field will bear fruit because the individuals responsible for eliciting the agricultural capacity do so in a sensitive manner.

The reward for adherence to covenant is not a this-worldly reward. In this world there are only legitimate consequences, and good ones at that, for living a life of good deeds and responsible behavior. To be satisfied with a little bit is to be satisfied a lot.

SIDRAH BE-MIDBAR
Levitic Demographics

The census of the Israelite community, the grand total of the Israelite population in the wilderness, is revealed in Sidrah Be-midbar. There is a separate count of all the tribes as well. This method of census-taking gives each tribal family a sense of its own importance, and an appreciation of its uniqueness within the community.

In this enumeration, the tribal sizes range anywhere from thirty-two thousand to seventy-four thousand males above the age of twenty. The tribe of Levi, when counted from the age of thirty and up, numbered only about eight and one-half thousand (Be-midbar 4:48). The count of the number of Levites from one month and up was only twenty-two thousand (Be-midbar 3:39). It is immediately obvious that the Levites did not proliferate at the same rate as the rest of the community of Israel.

Since the Levites were distinguished from the rest of the community by their work in the *Bet HaMikdash* and the sacred nature of their calling, it is puzzling why in fact this tribe had such a relatively low birthrate.

This question is addressed by Ramban. He suggests that the Levites did not fall for the original trap of Pharaoh and that they were able to avoid servitude in Egypt. The rest of Israel was afflicted through this intense servitude, but the more they were afflicted, the more they multiplied (Shemot 1:12). This was God's way of showing the Egyptians that God was more powerful. No matter how they attempted to control the numbers of the Israelite population, they would not succeed. Not only would they not succeed, their efforts would work in the reverse direction—Israel would actually multiply. However, the Levites, having not been included in the servitude, were also not part of this extraordinary multiplication process that was designed to blunt the designs of Pharaoh (Ramban, comment on Be-midbar 3:14).

There is a psychological dimension to the theologically oriented explanation of Ramban. Throughout the Israelite's stay in Egypt, when they were under threat, they persevered, refusing to buckle. Orders given to throw male children into the river were ignored at the risk of life. The Israelites also resorted to extraordinary measures once they sensed Pharaoh desired to destroy them by separating husbands from wives, thus making conjugal relations next to impossible and childbirth highly unlikely. What he could not achieve through direct edicts, Pharaoh attempted to achieve through indirect measures, which included a highly demanding workload with hardly any free time, and the relocation of husbands to places far from their homes. It is a tribute to the people of Israel, that they more than compensated. They went out of their way, undoubtedly having more children than they would have had under normal circumstances. However, the Levites, whose existence was not in jeopardy, did not feel the crisis and went about business as usual.

In the end, those who were subjected to intense affliction were able to look back at that period in their lives as one which yielded great fulfillment. On the other hand, those who lived through the situation in relative calm could look back at this period of time and only lament that now their population was quite sparse relative to that of other tribes within the community.

What happened to the Levites and the other tribes of Israel is also, for better or for worse, a profound lesson of history. While it would be ridiculous to welcome suffering and affliction at any time, it seems as if we have always had the great ability to rise to the occasion when under threat. But we have not fared nearly as well when circumstances were favorable and there was no apparent threat to communal viability.

SIDRAH NASO
We are Capable

The law of the *sotah*, the woman suspected of adultery, is followed by the law of the nazirite. This proximity raises the question What is the connection between the two? The Talmud states that it is to teach that whoever sees the *sotah* in her indignity should resolve to abstain from wine (Sotah 2a). This is a reference to the fact that the nazirite is forbidden to drink wine during the term of naziritism (Be-midbar 6:3).

What is the simple meaning of this talmudic comment? It is also difficult to understand why the Talmud would recommend abstaining from wine, considering that according to one view, the nazirite is considered a sinner precisely because he afflicted himself by abstaining from wine (Talmud, Nedarim 10a, to Be-midbar 6:11).

For every woman who is accused of adultery, there is a man who must share in her guilt if she is indeed guilty. The suspected male is not directly involved in the *sotah* process, since that process is primarily intended to effect reconciliation of the accused wife with her husband. Nevertheless, it should not be assumed that this man's actions are not to be taken seriously. There is a danger that the male population may be blasé about adultery. They may look upon it as merely reflecting the vulnerability of women. After all, they may say, men would never do such a thing. But the fact is that there were men who did precisely that. Otherwise, the *sotah* would never be in such a position.

It is dangerous when people who see wrongdoing cavalierly dismiss the possibility that they could do such wrong. It is much to be preferred that people acknowledge that under similar circumstances, they may do precisely as did this adulterous scoundrel. The sages projected this quite insightfully, by urging all those who see the *sotah* in her indignity to resolve to abstain from wine. When one drinks wine, one lets loose the inhibitions. Anything, including latent but previously controlled urges, may be unleashed. The symbolic gesture of abstaining from wine is a Rabbinic message to all who see the consequences of uncontrolled behavior. This message is that they are to take appropriate steps to assure they are never in a position wherein they may they lose control over their sensual capacities.

The sages saw the nazirite regulations as a counterbalance to the situation of the *sotah*. Rather than one-sidedly heaping responsibility on the *sotah* alone, the Torah, according to the Rabbinic comment concerning the juxtaposition of the law of the nazirite, points out a balance of blame and responsibility.

SIDRAH BE-HA'ALOTKHA
Capsule History

It is common knowledge that the Torah is divided into five books. However, according to the Talmud, there are actually seven books. What we know as the book of Be-midbar is really three books; the first part of Be-midbar, the last part, and the middle part (Shabbat 116a). The middle part is what subdivides the book of Be-midbar into three. However, that middle part is made up of only two verses.

These two verses read as follows: "And it was when the Ark traveled that Mosheh would say, 'Arise God, may your enemies be scattered, and let those that hate You flee from You.' And when the Ark rested, he would say, 'Return God, the myriads of the thousands of Israel'" (Be-midbar 10:35-36).

These two verses are sectioned off by an upside-down *nun* at both the beginning and the end. The fact that this forms an entire *sefer*, an entire book, is perplexing. Surely two verses cannot make for an entire book. Additionally, why are these two verses set off with an upside-down *nun*? They could have been set off by using any other inverted letter of the alphabet or without using any letters. Finally, if these two verses are so important, why are they inserted here?

The answer to the last question is already suggested by the commentaries. The section preceding the two verses speaks of an unfortunate event in Israel's sojourn in the wilderness, and the section immediately following the verses likewise deals with an unfortunate incident. In order to separate the two, these verses were inserted.

However, this only further complicates matters. If it were necessary to make a separation, so as to not be overwhelmed with a full string of unfortunate incidents, there is ample material available. Any of the mitzvot as described in detail could have been inserted. For example, the rules of the trumpets, which are in close proximity to these episodes, could have been inserted.

The two verses that form an entire book are employed in the regular liturgy whenever a Torah is taken out. The first verse is the lead sentence when the ark is opened. The second is the lead verse when the Torah is returned to the ark.

The first verse seems slightly paranoid. Why does Mosheh Rabbenu ask God to scatter God's enemies, precisely when the Ark travels forth? This prayer quite likely results from a combination of past experience and present insight. Israel was already attacked for no apparent reason just after it was redeemed from Egyptian bondage. Mosheh Rabbenu anticipated that the attack of Amalek was a harbinger of things to come. Israel would be constantly vulnerable to attack, precisely because of its allegiance to God. Mosheh Rabbenu recognized that whenever Israel traveled forth with its Torah code, it became susceptible to attack. Mosheh Rabbenu's prayer is that the enemies scatter, so that Israel can return with its full numbers. The myriads of the thousands should return complete, content, and able to resume their mission in life.

These verses are more than just two sentences. They are an entire book. They are the book of Jewish history. They are the capsule essence of what has happened to Israel throughout its turbulent existence. Wherever Israel went it was vulnerable. Wherever Israel went, the primary hope was not to become a victor over the vanquished; it was merely to return in peace with undiminished numbers, able to function adequately.

The upside-down *nun* thus begins to make a little more sense. The *nun* in Hebrew connotes *nefilah*, or falling. In battle, the objective of an army is to assure the fall of its enemy. However, the upside-down *nun* on either end of this book of Jewish history, imparts the message that our strategy is not to cause anyone's *nefilah*. We should just satisfy ourselves through having attained the opposite of *nefilah*, avoiding our own *nefilah*, as symbolized by the upside-down *nun*. Our strategy should not be to demolish and destroy. It should be to survive with as few casualties as possible.

But why is this complete book of Jewish history inserted where it is? The unfortunate incident immediately preceding concerns the fact that the Israelites had left the mountain of God. A midrashic commentary states that the people ran away from Mount Sinai as quickly as possible. They felt that they were already heavily burdened by having received so many commandments. They ran away in an attempt to avoid receiving more. They obviously saw adhering to God's word as a yoke, a yoke from which they attempted to escape. Immediately following this *sefer*, the Torah reports on the episode of the complainers, who likewise devised strategies to escape from the onerous burdens of their faith.

The insertion of this book between these two episodes is thus quite appropriate. Both these episodes have as a common denominator the feeling that living by God's word is an exacting task that is better avoided. The insertion of these verses between these two episodes contains a subtle message. It is that what Israel fails to appreciate, others seem to value. For, at bottom, the desire of Israel's enemies to destroy Israel is out of envy that Israel is so ennobled by its higher calling, a calling which it freely embraced.

The message to the people is clear. You run away from, and therefore deny, the value of that which everyone around clearly envies about you. The fact that your Torah is envied should be ample evidence to you of its worthwhileness and its enduring importance.

SIDRAH SHELAḤ
Israel as an Emotion

At the outset of Shelaḥ, God tells Mosheh to send men that they may search out the land of Canaan (Be-midbar 13:2). Rashi, commenting on the extra word *lekha* ("for you"), states that this is "According to your own judgment; I do not command you, but if you wish to do so, send them" (Rashi, comment on Be-midbar 13:2). In the words of the Talmud, "It pleased Mosheh well, but not the All-Present" (Sotah 34b).

Before the Jewish people entered the land of Canaan (Israel), they decided to send *meraglim*, spies, to explore the land and investigate the value of Eretz Yisrael for the people.

Seemingly, this was a legitimate undertaking. After all, a responsible person does not commit to a real estate proposition unless and until convinced it is a good deal. Yet, although Mosheh liked the idea, God's misgivings about the venture are abundantly clear.

These misgivings seem difficult to appreciate. Mosheh the faithful servant surely trusted God's judgment. His agreement to send the mission was not born of a lack of faith. Perhaps his motivation was to increase the people's excitement through a glowing report about the land. Why did this not meet with God's approval?

The search for an answer to this question leads to an understanding of the role of language in real life. We are under the impression that language is an avenue of communication between people. But, this being granted, language is not without its built-in faults. Consider the statement by the famous psychologist Rudolf Arnheim:

> I've found that as soon as you have a concept for something, you start to exclude it from the checkup of continued experience. If you do not constantly expose your concepts to experience they rapidly become rigid and paralyzed. They become lifeless clichés, fossils of experience.

Arnheim goes on to point out that the verbal concept is a shell placed over a certain experience. The great discoveries in each science came from people who ignored existing concepts in order to get back to the experience. Einstein, for example, was unable to speak until the age of three, and thus he developed an extraordinary feel for nonverbal concepts. Einstein wrote that his initial grasp of relativity was a kinesthetic image, a certain feeling he would get through his body.

In our own literature, we have examples of language transcendence which point to this idea. Thus, "The service of the Torah is greater than the study thereof" (Talmud, Berakhot 7b). Study is a word-language exercise; service is the real experience of Jewish dictates.

There was great reluctance to commit the Oral Tradition to writing. Only because of the danger that it might be forgotten was that tradition put down in writing. "It is better that one letter (prohibiting the writing of Oral Tradition) be uprooted than that the whole Torah be forgotten" (Talmud, Temurah 14b).

Oral Tradition, the language of life experience, is quite obviously an integral part of Jewish life, a part that was somewhat lost in the redaction of the Talmud. Even so, we still find many tales and statements in the Talmud which almost defy reason. These are attempts to transcend the concrete limitations of language, and it is in this context that they should be approached.

Experience, then, is much more a part of human endeavor than language. And, experience includes the actualizing of the senses, the feeling of emotion about an issue or ideal.

In such a vein, it is possible to appreciate the Heavenly reluctance regarding the exploration of the *meraglim*. Indeed, they might have come back with a glorious report, a position paper on Israel. But that would have reduced an emotive idea to sterile words. The people would have then entered Israel with their minds, but not with their whole beings.

Quite instructive is a comment of the Kli Yakar. He says that God preferred not *anashim* ("men"), rather *nashim* ("women"), who loved the land emotionally and would have come back only with an emotive statement about Israel.

Israel, then, is an experience. It is an experience beyond words and defying language; in a word, indescribable. No exploratory report could have maintained the emotive pitch of the land. Even today, the true lovers of Israel can hardly convey their feelings in words.

There is an emotive feeling toward Israel which transcends language, which cannot be chronicled, filmed, or reported. But because it cannot be concretized, it can never suffer the fate of concrete things. It can never be torn, withered, or destroyed.

SIDRAH KORAḤ
No More Defense

Mosheh Rabbenu did not have an easy time leading Israel through the wilderness. He had to contend with constant rebellions against God. But as the great leader he was, he continually went back to God arguing on behalf of Israel.

However, when Koraḥ and his cohorts rebelled against Mosheh and Aharon, Mosheh fell on his face (Be-midbar 16:4). Rashi, citing midrashic sources, says that Mosheh was able to argue on behalf of Israel following the Golden Calf episode, following their complaints, and even following the episode of the *meraglim*, (those who came back from Israel with a negative report about entering the promised land). However, when it came to the rebellion of Koraḥ, Mosheh was weakened and felt helpless to intervene with God on behalf of the community.

This comment seems quite problematic. Is it suggesting that Mosheh Rabbenu was more concerned about his own honor than about God's honor? The implication of Rashi is that Mosheh Rabbenu was eager to defend Israel when Israel rebelled against God, but that he found himself enervated and unable to defend Israel when they rebelled against him and Aharon. Does this make sense?

It is also difficult to believe that Mosheh Rabbenu, the most humble of all human beings, would be so meticulous when it came to his own honor. In fact just the opposite is true. When the rebellion became more intense, Mosheh Rabbenu did not stand on ceremony. Instead, he went up to directly approach the combatants and hope that thereby the rebellion could be quietened (Be-midbar 17:25).

One must therefore seek a meaning beyond what is suggested from a superficial reading of the midrashic comment cited by Rashi. It may be that the arguments mustered by Mosheh Rabbenu to defend Israel, different though they may have been relative to the circumstances, were all rooted in his appreciation that the people were wrestling with the ghosts of the past. A people cannot live in a pagan environment for hundreds of years and remain unaffected. Mosheh Rabbenu's defense of the people was rooted in his understanding that their conception of God's majesty and power had not yet become fully integrated. How else can you explain their rebelling almost immediately after having witnessed the great miracle of the Exodus. Mosheh Rabbenu thus felt justified in defending the people's seemingly inexcusable behavior.

Now, however, with the rebellion of Koraḥ, Mosheh Rabbenu was totally frustrated. Here he is trying to defend the people on the basis of their efforts to shake off and thrust away the foreign influences that had penetrated. But how can he justify all these arguments to God, if God points out to him that they rebelled not only against God but also against Mosheh. God can understand and appreciate why they would rebel against God, since they did not yet understand the idea of God as architect of the world, all-powerful and all-knowing. But the rebellion of Koraḥ could not be similarly dismissed with such an argument.

The rebellion of Koraḥ was merely a power struggle with no theological implications. It was a crude attempt by one segment of the population, which had significant support, to try to gain power. It was an attempt to gain power in callous disregard of all that Mosheh Rabbenu had done for them. Mosheh Rabbenu realized that because this rebellion was against him, he could no longer justify Israel's rebellion against God on the theological grounds that he had used previously. The people proved that their rebellion was not because of ghosts of the past that were haunting them. Their rebellion was rooted in problematic character patterns that were expressing themselves in the present. It is for this reason that Mosheh fell down on his face.

SIDRAH ḤUKKAT
The Red Heifer Paradox

The Torah introduces the ritual of the red heifer by labeling it a statute, a legislation which is beyond rational understanding (Be-midbar 19:2). Shlomoh HaMelekh said of the red heifer that he thought that he would acquire wisdom, but this was beyond his grasp (Midrash, Be-midbar Rabbah 19:3). What specifically in the red heifer ritual is beyond rational comprehension? It is the fact that the ashes of the red heifer, when sprinkled upon the one who is *tamay* (ritually distant, for having come in contact with a corpse), render that individual *tahor* (ritually attached and able to take part in specific religious functions which demand a state of being *tahor*). These same ashes render all those who come in contact with them, from the *kohen* who did the sprinkling to the one who gathers the ashes, *tamay* for a short period of time.

How is it that the ashes which allow the person who is *tamay* to become *tahor* at the same time cause the one who is *tahor* to thereby become *tamay*? This is the *parah*-dox of the red heifer legislation, which places it beyond comprehension.

There may be a pointed message that is projected in this seemingly incomprehensible regulation. A doctor who treats a patient, and who through thorough examination is able to determine precisely the nature of the person's malaise, will then prescribe the proper medication and send the patient on the way to recovery. The doctor will then usually be careful to wash the hands before examining the next patient, in order not to transmit germs from one patient to the next. In medicine, one can see quite readily that the process of curing carries with it the necessity of cleansing the one who renders the cure. This is understandable; one would not dare consider it beyond comprehension. It is taken as a given that the process of curing involves risk-taking by doctors, who, to protect other patients, must cleanse themselves before approaching others.

What is true in a medical sense is suggested in the spiritual sense, via the paradoxical legislation of the red heifer. All those involved in the purification, or rendering *tahor*, of the person who is *tamay*, are themselves rendered *tamay* in the process, as previously mentioned. What is hereby suggested is that individuals in the helping fields, who aid others to regain the state of being that they desire, whether it be in a physical sense, a mental sense, or a spiritual sense, have in the process become affected.

There is always a danger that an individual who regularly helps others may begin to feel a degree of exaggerated self-importance. After all, everyone is dependent on him or her, so that individual must be extra special. The very act of helping others can be detrimental to the helper. Through the red heifer legislation, a balance is injected. The helper is told that in the act of helping one is rendered unfit to be involved in activities for which one must be *tahor*; one is *tamay* for a short period of time.

During this period of time, it is hoped that the individual will contemplate why the act of helping has in fact caused personal harm. It is to be hoped that the message will be driven home that helping others should not be seen as a mark of superiority which can induce arrogance. Helping should be done with humility and should not allow for any value distortion.

SIDRAH BALAK
Hate and Envy

The saga of Balak begins with a report of his seeing all that Israel had done to the Amorites. The one-sidedness of Balak's approach is immediately apparent, in that, as has been pointed out in leading commentaries, he saw all that Israel had done to the Amorites but refused to see what the Amorites had done to Israel. Israel defeated the Amorites in battle, not through an aggressive war, but in self-defence after having been attacked by them. But this important fact was neglected by Balak, as it has been "neglected" in our own times by Israel's adversaries in the Middle East, specifically with regard to the Six-Day War, and the territories captured by Israel in an obvious war of self-defence against aggression and the attempt to drive Israel into the sea.

Balak is in dread of Israel. He is afraid that they will lick up all that is around him as the ox licks up the grass from the field (Be-midbar 22:4).

Balak hires a public relations expert by the name of Bilam, whom he hopes will curse and vilify Israel so that Israel may become an international pariah. Balak obviously hopes that once Israel is established as a pariah, he will gain international support for his attempts to destroy Israel. The strategy of Balak has reached into the twentieth century. It has found its way into the chambers of the United Nations, where Israel's adversaries have used precisely these tactics to isolate Israel within the world community and, they hope, thus make Israel "deserving of destruction."

In the end, Balak's strategy does not work. Bilam's attempts to curse Israel do not come out in the way that Balak had hoped. The intended curses come out as blessings. This was effected by God's intervention.

However, one can at the same time see in this a human component. Bilam, in agreeing to carry out Balak's wishes, obviously shared Balak's hatred for Israel. But often, envy is the root of hatred, the envy of what other people have but you do not; you hate these others for having what you would like to have but are not fortunate enough to possess. Bilam saw a community that was tranquil, that was focused, that was directed. This he envied. The hatred for Israel was related to Israel's strong sense of purpose, which remained firm despite the ups and downs of the community's turbulent relationship with God and Mosheh Rabbenu in the wilderness.

What Bilam intended as a curse came out as a blessing. This suggests that the hatred of Israel's enemies toward Israel is often envy of the good that Israel possesses. This hatred tells Israel that it must be doing something right. Otherwise it would simply be ignored. We continue to recall Bilam's observations, since, though they are infused with hate, they are eloquent testimony to the many qualities of Israel we should love and cherish.

SIDRAH PINḤAS
True Pioneers

Even before they entered the Land of Israel, the people of Israel were given instructions about how to divide the land. No one was to be given any extra privileges. The land was to be divided according to number. "To the more you shall give the more inheritance, and to the fewer you shall give the less inheritance . . . " (Be-midbar 26:54).

What does the statement that the more will get the more inheritance and the less will get less inheritance mean? Surely if each one gets the same amount, then there is no issue of more or less. Sifri and the Talmud (Baba Batra 117a-b) give an interesting twist to this equation.

According to the view of Rabbi Yoshiyah, the land was divided according to the number of Israelites who left Egypt. A family with five sons when leaving Egypt, but with ten or more sons upon entry into Israel, would would be given land based on the family of five. A family which left Egypt with ten sons, and came into Israel with less than ten, would be given land based on the family of ten. All depended on how many children there were in the family at the time of the Exodus.

This is a unique way of dividing property, since normally one thinks in terms of dividing property according to those present at the time of the distribution rather than according to the numbers of those present many years earlier.

Obviously, this procedure is intended to bestow a significantly greater reward on those who left Egypt than on those who persevered through the wilderness (*midbar*). Those who raised children in Egypt did so at great personal sacrifice and out of pure faith. There was no promise of any reward, no prospect that the greater the number of children the better off the family would be. Quite the contrary; each child was in jeopardy, a potential candidate for being enslaved, or even killed. Nevertheless, the people kept their faith in God and never gave up hope that they would eventually be redeemed from the excruciating subjugation.

Having left Egypt and having been redeemed into freedom, the people were preparing to enter the promised land. where there were great prospects for a bountiful yield from the fertile land. Since in agriculture, increasing the number of people working the soil usually increases the yield, it would have been to the advantage of any family to have more children. More children meant more workers and, therefore, greater productivity. A family that had more children in the wilderness in anticipation of the entry into Israel did not necessarily do so as an act of faith; it may have been more a matter of practicality.

The Torah, in dividing the land according to the number of those who left Egypt, rewards the true pioneers, those who at great personal risk continued to affirm their responsibilities, who continued to obey the injunction to be fruitful and multiply.

Even as the people enter Israel, they are taught a very important lesson. That lesson is that they owe whatever present fulfillments they will enjoy to the dedication of their forebears, who at great personal sacrifice made sure there would be a tomorrow. We enjoy the tomorrow, but we never forget the yesterday.

SIDRAH MATTOT
Built-in Protection

"Whoever causes the multitude to be virtuous, no sin shall come through that person, but one who causes the multitude to sin will not be given the opportunity to repent" (Mishnah, Avot 5:21). According to this statement in the Mishnah, an individual who leads the community, who enhances and uplifts that community, need not worry that the community may be led astray. Leaders who are dedicated to the community are obviously concerned that they may err at one point or another, that they may inadvertently mislead the community. Such a fear is likely to dissuade well-meaning individuals from assuming leadership roles; they would fear the potentially dire consequences of misleading the people. The Mishnah here assures these sensitive individuals that they need not worry.

The proof for this is none other than Mosheh Rabbenu. Mosheh was himself virtuous and caused the multitude to be virtuous. Therefore the virtuousness of the multitude is ascribed to him, as it is written, "he performed the righteousness of God and His judgment with Israel" (Devarim 33:21). Mosheh Rabbenu is hereby given the credit for the righteous behavior of Israel. At the same time, the verse refers to a situation Mosheh Rabbenu confronted, in which there was a great potential for error—the episode involving the tribes of Reuven and Gad and half the tribe of Menasheh.

The tribes of Reuven and Gad and half the tribe of Menasheh came to Mosheh Rabbenu asking to settle on the other side of the Jordan. They desired to settle there because they had many cattle and it was an area that was ideal for cattle grazing. At first Mosheh Rabbenu was suspicious and therefore reluctant. He feared that this was a ruse by these two and one-half tribes to avoid military service. If they were not to enter the Land of Israel, they could excuse themselves from whatever conflicts might be involved in the process, by saying that they were not going onto that side of the Jordan anyway. Mosheh Rabbenu feared that such distancing would create ill will within the community and would ultimately sever these two and one-half tribes from the rest of the community; he feared that they would be lost to Israel.

Some might question why Mosheh Rabbenu reacted so angrily, but his experience with some of the rebellious episodes was reason enough to make him suspect there was something amiss. Indeed, when the tribes come back after Mosheh Rabbenu's initial expressed outrage, they say to Mosheh that they will build enclosures for their cattle and then cities for their children. After having done so, they say, they will join the community in whatever battles they may confront.

Mosheh Rabbenu, sensing this value distortion, corrects them on their priorities. He tells them that they should first build cities for their children and then enclosures for their cattle. Children are much more important than animals (see Rashi's comment on Be-midbar 32:16). It is not out of bounds to suggest that Mosheh Rabbenu had already sensed there was some value distortion in the request and therefore reacted angrily.

Apparently the message came through. The two and one-half tribes offer to do their part. Mosheh Rabbenu then agrees to their request. He allows them to eventually settle on the other side of the Jordan, providing that they help their brethren settle in Israel (Be-midbar 32:1-32).

The verse concerning the fact that Mosheh performed the righteousness of God and His judgment with Israel refers to this episode. The danger inherent in the request of the two and one-half tribes is readily apparent, as was obvious to Mosheh Rabbenu, judging by his initial reaction. The final resolution of this request made everyone happy. It allowed these tribes to specialize in the area that was most consistent with their own economic circumstance, but it did not compromise their involvement with the community.

When leadership is like that of Mosheh Rabbenu, concerned with enhancing community and uplifting it, and totally devoid of any desire for personal aggrandizement, then such leadership is able to steer the community through even the most delicate of dilemmas. Dedicated, transcending leadership yields commensurately noble results.

SIDRAH MASEI
Honorable Mention

In the forty years the Israelites sojourned in the wilderness, they made forty-two stops. The precise locale for each of these forty-two stops is spelled out in detail in the Torah (Be-midbar 31:1-49).

The travels are preceded by the following preamble: "And Mosheh wrote their going forth stage by stage, by the command of God, and these are their stages at their goings forth" (Be-midbar 33:2). According to the literal translation of the text, the words "by the command of God" refer to their going forth stage by stage. It means that the going forth stage by stage was by God's command. Ibn Ezra seems to adopt this reading of the text. Ramban, however, strongly disagrees with Ibn Ezra on this. He claims that it is already mentioned in other places that the people traveled and camped according to the word of God. It is therefore unnecessary to repeat this once again.

Ramban therefore suggests that the words "by the command of God," refer to the first part of the verse, "And Mosheh wrote . . . " According to the version of Ramban, the passage, in translation, would read as follows: "And Mosheh wrote by the command of God, their going forth stage by stage, and these are their stages at their goings forth."

Ramban, following Rashi, suggests that the command of God in this regard was to show the kindness of God. Even though Israel was burdened with having to wander in the wilderness for forty years, it was not as if they had no rest during that time. They did wander, but they only had forty-two stops in the forty years. And, as Rashi further develops (Be-midbar 31:1), in the middle thirty-eight years they had only twenty stops.

But if that were the only reason for writing the stops, it would have been much simpler to just mention that during Israel's sojourn in the wilderness they only made forty-two stops, with fourteen stops in the first year, eight stops in the last year, and only twenty stops in the middle thirty-eight years. Why was it necessary to mention the names of all the places? Midrash Be-midbar Rabbah (23:3) suggests that these cities are mentioned because they welcomed the Israelites. Putting the observation of Ramban together with this midrash, God ordered Mosheh Rabbenu to list the cities where the people camped, in order to give these cities credit for their hospitality.

One may argue that these cities actually did nothing for Israel. After all, these were not established cities. These were points on the map. There were no walls to the cities; no permission was needed in order to enter these places. What then did these cities do to deserve the credit?

The answer is that they did nothing but still deserve the credit. God instructs Mosheh Rabbenu to write these cities down, because on his own Mosheh Rabbenu probably would not have listed them, for the reason just mentioned. But God is here transmitting, via Mosheh Rabbenu, an important lesson to the community of Israel. We have an obligation to acknowledge the good that is done for us even if we can rationalize away the good by saying that it would have happened anyway or that the good was never intended or any other such excuse. If good things happen to us, we should be grateful and not look for excuses to avoid saying thank you. The cities get honorable mention because however indirectly they contributed to Israel's comfort, they are nevertheless deserving of thanks.

SIDRAH DEVARIM
Dimensions of Leadership

At the very outset of Sedra Devarim, we are offered a keen insight into the dynamics of leadership within the Israelite community. In the fortieth year, after Mosheh Rabbenu had led the Israelites to victory against the forces of Siḥon and Og (Devarim 1:3-4), "Mosheh began to explain this Torah" (1:4). The Torah, or at least parts of it, had already been presented to the Israelite community beforehand. This was certainly not the first time that Mosheh was transmitting the will of God to the people.

However, this may have been the first time that Mosheh succeeded in being able to *explain* the Torah to the people. Prior to this moment, the Torah was transmitted in a matter-of-fact manner; now the Torah was being explained to the people. Why was this elucidation possible only now?

Mosheh's explaining of the Torah to the people came on the heels of a dramatic victory against the forces of Siḥon and Og. Perhaps the people now saw Mosheh Rabbenu in a new light. He was no longer perceived as the ivory tower academic who was not part of the real world. This scholar was also a mighty warrior. He knew the intricacies of the intellect, yet he could also fight a military battle, and triumph. Mosheh became a hero and earned a new respect from the people. He was a one-dimensional person no more; Mosheh was now appreciated as an individual who understood life in its totality.

Beforehand, Mosheh Rabbenu could only transmit the word of God; now that he gained the confidence of the people, they were eager to hear the rationale, the full explanation, of the Torah. Mosheh Rabbenu was now able to explain the Torah, because the people were now much more willing and eager to hear those explanations.

Of course, Mosheh Rabbenu had already well established his credentials as one who could stand up to an aggressor. He did this in the confrontation with Pharaoh and, later, in the confrontation with Amalek. But the people, having spent forty years with Mosheh Rabbenu in the wilderness, developed a perception of Mosheh that was much more limited and parochial. It was through the confrontation with Sihon and Og that they realized how they had erred, that in fact Mosheh Rabbenu did not just now become a warrior, able to stand up and fight for the community, that he had always been this way. This episode just brought back the memories of the past and jolted the people into realizing how much they had been mistaken in their perception.

K'tav V'Kabbalah makes some fascinating comments concerning Mosheh Rabbenu's teaching Israel. Rashi observes that the verse stating that Mosheh explained the Torah means that he transmitted the Torah in seventy languages. K'tav V'Kabbalah refuses to take this literally. He asks what would be gained from this multilingual transmission? Rather, Rashi uses the term "language" in the sense of facets. Mosheh Rabbenu transmitted the multiple facets and meanings of the Torah to the people. Before, Mosheh was a conduit transmitting messages. Now, he was a pedagogue explaining the full meaning of the messages.

Mosheh Rabbenu "began" to explain. The word "began" is the translation of the biblical word *ho'eel*. According to K'tav V'Kabbalah, *ho'eel* means energized. Mosheh Rabbenu was now energized to fully explain the Torah. To enlarge on this, it may be that just now, Mosheh Rabbenu sensed that Israel was more than willing, it was actually eager to hear what he had to say. Because of their newly found appreciation of their leader, Israel was actively ready to absorb the Torah. Mosheh Rabbenu, sensing this, became energized, invigorated to the task of teaching, as would any true teacher with hungry students. Mosheh Rabbenu was, at once, the master teacher and the commander-in-chief. He combined power and resolve with insight and wisdom.

The model of leader in the mold of Mosheh Rabbenu should be a multidimensional person, able to address all the needs of the community—physical, spiritual, emotional, and political. Unfortunately, in our generation, we have seen a great compartmentalization in regard to these functions of leadership. The secular community has one set of leaders, the religious community has another set. It is difficult to think of any individual whose leadership capacities are such that they can magnetically attract individuals from both the religious and secular portions of the community.

As in the time of Mosheh Rabbenu, the secular feel that religious leaders do not address themselves to the needs of the secular community, and the religious feel that the secular leaders certainly are not concerned with the religious community. Hence, we face the danger of a partitioning of the community into different constituencies with different leaders. A leader in the mold of Mosheh, who combines scholarship and commitment with concern for the multidimensional facets of Jewish existence, is sorely needed in this most critical time in Jewish history. Such a leader is more likely to emerge if the community of student-scholars is encouraged to be part of the total community, rather than locking itself away from the rest of the community within the walls of the house of study.

Only when—and if—the Jewish community is fortunate enough to have as its leader one who has the attributes of Mosheh can we begin in earnest the desperately necessary process of "explaining," of enlightening the community with the multifaceted wisdom of the Torah.

SIDRAH VA-ETHANNAN
Conditional Destiny

Judaism places a great emphasis on self-preservation, on taking care of oneself, avoiding bad habits and dangerous practices that can compromise one's health or one's life. The full text of the verse that is often cited as the basis for this is "Be exceedingly heedful of yourselves, for you saw no likeness at all on the day that God spoke to you in Horev out of the midst of the fire" (Devarim 4:15).

The portion of the verse that suggests the precept of self-preservation is quite obvious. It inheres in the first part of the passage, admonishing the community "Be exceedingly heedful of yourselves . . ." However, the remainder of the verse remains quite perplexing. It seems to offer an explanation, namely, that we should do so because we saw no likeness of God when God appeared from out of the fire at Horev to transmit the Torah to the Israelite community. Bluntly, what does the one have to do with the other? In what way is self-preservation related to the fact that God did not appear in any form? This seems to be totally irrelevant to the obligation.

To gain a proper understanding of this passage, it is essential to reflect on the implications of the fact that God did not appear in a form. We know, as a basic theological principle, that God has no form. This is a clearly enunciated concept (Maimonides, Laws of the Foundations of the Torah [*Hilkhot Yesoday HaTorah*] 1:8).

However, even though God does not have any form or likeness, a likeness could be transmitted to the people by God in order to project some particular message. The fact that the people might perceive an arm of God intervening in a conflict or a voice of God transmitting a message does not automatically mean "God has an arm" or "God has a throat." In other words, what the people are shown is not necessarily what is. It could be true that God has no shape or form and yet be possible for the people to experience such a shape or form. This could occur simply because God desires it to occur.

However, at Sinai, when the Commandments were given, God did not manifest any shape or form. The question that remains is why God chose not to project any likeness. It is conceivable that God wanted to project a message by not appearing in any likeness. The people would not see any shape, they would not experience any finite form. Instead, they would perceive in the abstract.

God was thus telling the people that through that which was transmitted to them, through *their* adherence to the Commandments, they who would give their lives the proper shape and form. In other words, God does not project finitude or absolutely nonnegotiable borders. The people, through the way of life that they espouse, can stretch any preconceived limits or reduce them.

With this as background, the verse becomes more clear. We are told to be exceedingly heedful of ourselves. We are told thereby that the length of one's life is not a finite, preordained number of years, but is rather a variable number of years, dependent on how we take care of ourselves. The individual who may have been allotted seventy or seventy-five years, but has abused life, may therefore live a much shorter time. The individual who may have been allocated only forty-five or fifty years, but has carefully nurtured and respected that life, may extend that allotted number of years. Taking care of ourselves only makes sense if the caretaking has a direct impact on the quantity and quality of our years. It is in this context that the balance of the passage should be read.

We are to take heed of ourselves, to give our lives extended borders, because God chose not to appear in a finite shape. God chose to leave the shaping of our lives to us, as if to indicate that the destiny of our years is conditional upon how we take care of those years. We have no right to hide behind abuse by saying *"Vos is bashert is bashert"* — whatever is destined is destined. It is true that we may begin with some unknown destiny, but we can subtract from it or add to it depending on how we choose to live.

SIDRAH EKEV
Land of Opportunity

Before he departs from the scene, Mosheh Rabbenu delivers a lengthy discourse recapitulating the history of the Israelite community. In his discourse he directs some particularly blistering remarks to the community. One such remark concerns Israel's entrenchment in the Land of Israel.

Mosheh Rabbenu admonishes the people that they should not believe that they are being given the Land of Israel because they are righteousness or because other nations are wicked. Instead, it is a combination of (1) the unworthiness of other nations, which would ultimately have led to their eviction anyway, and (2) the fulfillment of a promise that was given to the Patriarchs of the Israelite community, Avraham, Yiẓḥak, and Yaakov (Devarim 9:4-5). It is perplexing that Mosheh Rabbenu should resort to such harsh talk in his address to the community just days before his departure. Why did he speak in such blunt terms?

Mosheh Rabbenu obviously had a message to deliver. He wanted to impress upon the people two very important facts. The first was that the Israelite claim to the land of Israel is not based on moral superiority. The Israelites do not gain legal title to the land because they are nice. If title were to be transferred for such a reason, then all possession would become arbitrary; individuals would be able to dispossess others from their homes or their farms simply because they were not behaving nicely. Legal possession must be based on a legal claim, not on a moral judgment. Therefore, said Mosheh Rabbenu to the people, your claim to Israel is absolute. It is a promise that was made by God to your ancestors. Since God, who has created the world, owns the world, God has the right to choose to whom to give the land.

Secondly, says Mosheh Rabbenu, the fact of your history is that you are not morally superior, that you are not imbued with righteousness. You should not feel that your entry into Israel is testimony to your moral superiority. What Mosheh Rabbenu intended with this was to forestall the possibility of complacency developing within the community after his departure. He understood that it would be quite easy for the people to assume that since God had given them the land, God was obviously making a judgment about their deservedness. Hence, they could be smug about themselves and thereby neglect their moral development.

To underscore and prove this point, Mosheh Rabbenu says, "And you should know that it is not for your righteousness that God, your God, gives you this good land to take it into possession, for you are a stiff-necked people" (Devarim 9:6). Mosheh Rabbenu offers the people proof that they are far removed from righteousness. The proof is in the fact that the people are obstinate, stiff-necked. Sforno develops this point, indicating that the stiff-necked person, the obstinate one, makes up his or her mind and goes along with whatever decision has been made internally, refusing to listen to the views of others, refusing to follow the leadership of those who may be better informed and better advised. This was a problem that Mosheh Rabbenu faced continually during the forty arduous years he led the people after the Exodus. The obstinacy that Israel displayed during those years was proof positive to Mosheh Rabbenu of the gaps that still remained in Israel's development. So, Mosheh Rabbenu, ever the educator, alerts the people that going into Israel is less a statement of their existing character and more a character development opportunity.

SIDRAH RE'EH
Constructive Response

The entire community of Israel are considered to be God's children. "You are children of the Lord [God] your God . . ." (Devarim 14:1). The Talmud (Kiddushin 36a) reports a difference of opinion among the sages concerning who are actually included in this verse. In the view of Rabbi Yehudah, only those who behave as children, namely those who adhere to the words of God the parent, are embraced with the appellation "Children of God." However, in the view of Rabbi Meir, no matter how the children behave, they are still considered children of God. Normally, in a dispute between Rabbi Yehudah and Rabbi Meir, the view of Rabbi Yehudah prevails, but in this instance the view of Rabbi Meir prevails. Torah Temimah on this verse suggests that Rabbi Yehudah eventually embraced the view of Rabbi Meir.

The remainder of this verse, which begins with the thought that every member of the Israelite community is a child of God, reads as follows: "you shall not cut yourselves, nor make a bald patch between your eyes for the dead." The Torah here forbids the pagan practice of making incisions on one's body at the death of a close friend or relative.

The preamble to the prohibition is itself instructive. If in fact we are all one big happy family, then it is quite likely that we will take very seriously the death of anyone within the community. Indeed, we should lament the death of anyone within the community. However, we should not lament to an extreme.

We are all one big, happy, interrelated family, and each of us needs the other. This is at once a cause for lamenting the departed, and for being sensitive to the survivors. It is ridiculous and absurd to lament the death of one individual by inducing the partial death of a survivor or survivors by taking away more flesh from this earth. The response to death should be a recommitment to life; it certainly should not be to inflict further wounds upon the community. We glorify the deceased through the good deeds that are inspired by the desire to perpetuate the memory of the deceased.

This verse is not only a prohibition of cutting one's self (Talmud, Yevamot 13b); it is also understood as a prohibition of splitting up the community into disparate groups (Talmud, Yevamot 14a): *Lo titgodedu*, "You shall not cut yourself," or "You shall not cut the community into different bands (*agudot*)." When a leader of the community passes away, it may be the natural desire of the community to perpetuate the memory of that leader through following that individual's ways.

Often however, as the Talmud indicates, the ways of one departed may differ from the ways of another departed. The ways of Hillel are not the ways of Shammai. A significant portion may wish to honor Hillel's memory, while another portion may desire to honor Shammai's memory. But the memory of the deceased is not honored if it is the cause for communal disintegration. The overriding feature of the communal response to the passing of anyone must be that it operates in the context of harmony. If Hillel's views are the accepted norm, we do not honor Shammai's memory by imposing Shammai's views and thus dividing the community.

According to this talmudic reading, the verse is understood as follows: Since we are all children of God, when an individual within the community, one of the family of children, passes away, our reaction should not be an extreme reaction, either extreme in a spiritual sense or extreme in the physical sense. The extreme in a spiritual sense manifests itself in divisiveness; the extreme in a physical sense manifests itself in making bald patches on the face. Both of these are absurd responses which pervert the memory of the deceased.

Since we are part of one happy family, our reaction to a loss within the family should be to strengthen personal resolve and at the same time to enhance the community; to assure that the community is integrated and united. Preserving the future is the best way to honor the past.

SIDRAH SHOFETIM
Leadership—Ins and Outs

The ruler of the Jewish community, its king, was given greater obligations than the general population, since the king, as leader, had unique responsibilities. One such obligation was that the king had to possess two Torah scrolls. "And it shall be when he sits upon the throne of his kingdom, that he shall write a double copy of this Torah . . . " (Devarim 17:18). The king was obliged to lead—but not to lead indiscriminately. The king too was bound to the Torah and was impressed with this reality through the aforementioned biblical obligation.

The Talmud indicates that the two Torah scrolls were for different needs. One was stored away in the king's treasures, while the king would go out and return with the other. The one Torah was fixed; the other, portable.

Tosafot, commenting on the talmudic view that the Torah with which the king went out and came in was in the form of an amulet tied to the arm (Sanhedrin 21b), suggests a fascinating interpretation of this verse.

Obviously, it is hard to imagine the king carrying an entire Torah on his arm. Tosafot suggests that the *Torah* referred to was merely the Ten Commandments. Since there are 613 letters in the Ten Commandments, corresponding to the 613 Commandments, it is therefore also called a Torah.

The Torah here projects the reality of leadership. A leader, a shaper of community, a king or a rabbi, must be steeped in Torah knowledge. The king's home must contain the Torah in its entirety. However, a communal leader cannot stay at home. The knowledge the leader gains at home in the study of the Torah must be shared with the public. The Torah must be the anchor of the community, but must also be portable. The king must be able to carry the Torah to all of the people in his kingdom.

Additionally, the Talmud, on the basis of the words *v'khatav lo* ("[the King] shall write for himself"), deduces that the king cannot make use of a Torah that may have been bequeathed by his father. This regulation also applies to the entire community. Every member of the community is obliged to write a Torah, an obligation that cannot be fulfilled with a Torah inherited from one's parents (Devarim 31:19; Sanhedrin 21b). The king is here singled out for special mention—he must have two Torah scrolls, each new and uniquely his own.

One may wonder why the Torah insists on this. After all, an inherited scroll would carry with it warm memories and would be most meaningful, helping the king to feel connected to his parents or grandparents and to follow in the noble traditions of the past.

It is indeed the case that the king, if fortunate enough to succeed a worthy parent, should follow that example. However, each generation has different needs and unique circumstances. Thus the king cannot merely say, This is the way my father did it, therefore this is the way I will do it. The Torah does not change, but situations do. The Torah has unique responses to each unique situation. The king, who must live in the present, needs to learn in his own portals from his own permanent Torah. Then, imbued with the knowledge gained, he must step out into the public arena and apply what he has learned to the unique situation of his people, with the portable Torah that is uniquely his.

SIDRAH KI TEZE
Maintaining the Sources

Sidrah Ki Teze contains many rules of conduct, few as interesting and instructive as that concerning the bird's nest. This regulation establishes that if an individual is confronted with a bird's nest containing young birds or eggs and the mother is sitting upon the young birds or eggs, it is prohibited to take the mother with the young. Instead, the mother must be set free; only then may the young be taken (Devarim 22:6-7).

What is the rationale for this commandment? Ramban asserts that having mercy on the birds is not the reason. Mercy is involved, but it is in the desire to inculcate the feeling of mercifulness in the individual. The individual is therefore instructed not to take the mother with the young. The mitzvah, then, is an exercise in mercifulness for the individual, not the birds.

However, if this is the case, then taking the mother away may actually be less than a merciful gesture. It would be reasonable to assume that the mother would want to be with the young. Sending the mother away in the face of such awareness seems to be cruel.

Ramban further suggests that this legislation may be directed to the overriding importance of preservation of the species. It would be singularly insensitive to the species if one were to simultaneously take the source and the fruit, the mother and the children, and use them for personal gain in whatever way. Such total destruction shows no sensitivity to the need to maintain the species. The Torah therefore allowed the taking of the young but insisted that the mother, who brings forth and nurtures the young, be sent away unharmed.

The mitzvah as spelled out in the Torah concludes with a promise: "in order that it shall go well with you and you shall enjoy length of days" (Devarim 22:7). This promise contains a rarely used biblical expression, one that indicates almost a natural cause-and-effect relationship. The individual who respects nature, who is ever sensitive to the source of food supply, will through that caution and care assure that the food supply will be maintained. With the food supply being maintained, the individual will likely live a longer life. An individual who abuses nature, who destroys the natural supply of food at the source, will one day wake up to find that there is no food available because the supply lines have been cut. The bird's nest legislation thus impresses upon us the need to respect nature even as we glean from it.

There is another commandment in which the Torah steps out on a limb and promises longevity. This promise is made in the commandment to honor one's parents (Devarim 5:16). The promise of long life in the commandment to honor one's parents is the spiritual counterpart to the physical promise in the bird's nest legislation. We honor and respect our parents; they are our life source. Even as we embark upon the search for self-fulfillment, we dare not tread over our life source. Instead, we must integrate our search for the self, our desire for fulfillment, with respect for those who made it possible for us to embark on the search. It is only through our appreciating the source of our existence and behaving respectfully toward that source that we can have a happy life, a life blessed in quantity and in quality.

Preservation of our physical life source brings with it the promise of a continual food supply and hence a long life. Preservation of our spiritual life source brings with it the promise of a life of tranquility and blessedness, a longevity in which each day is profoundly valued.

SIDRAH KI TAVO
Roots of Thanksgiving

The bringing of the first fruits to Jerusalem was a meaningful occasion, that was imbued with a sense of history through the recitation of the prescribed formula of thanksgiving. The thanksgiving formula was not just a simple acknowledgment; it covered the entire scope of Israelite history. It begins with the attempts of Lavan the Aramean to destroy Yaakov, continues with the enslavement in Egypt, and concludes with the deliverance from slavery and the entry into the Land of Israel, where the people were able to make full use of the fertile yield. This formula was recited by one who brought the first fruits to the Temple in Jerusalem (Devarim 26:2-10).

True thanksgiving must be more than a perfunctory exercise and the recitation of a clichéd phrase. True thanksgiving must project a profound appreciation for all the ingredients that make possible the celebration of the present moment.

The thanksgiving begins with a simple statement, "An Aramean is trying to destroy my father . . . " (Devarim 26:5). Though this is a reference to a past episode, the confrontation of Lavan and Yaakov, the expression here appears in the present tense. This implies that the type of threat Lavan presented to the existence of Israel is not merely relegated to the past; rather it is an ongoing threat, demanding continuing vigilance.

Lavan's was a peculiar and unique assault on Israelite tradition. His attack on Yaakov was subtle. He projected himself as a friend; indeed he was an uncle to Yaakov. He tried to gain Yaakov's confidence, at the same time concealing his desire to destroy Yaakov.

Lavan made life miserable for Yaakov after he became his father-in-law. He probably sensed from the outset that the values of his son-in-law were radically different from his own. Inevitably, without any intervention, Yaakov's wives—Lavan's daughters—and their children would part company from Lavan and his undesirable philosophy.

Lavan cleverly manipulated the working conditions and obligations of Yaakov in order to prevent Yaakov from ever gaining any real independence. Lavan hoped that by keeping Yaakov dependent he would assure that his daughters and grandchildren would always remain with him. Thus he would keep alive the possibility that he might win them over to his way of life.

The plan, sly and subtle as it was, did not work. In spite of all the constraints imposed upon Yaakov by Lavan, Yaakov succeeded in amassing enough wealth to enable his entire family to leave. As soon as this was possible, Yaakov and his family made a radical break from the idolatrous environment of Lavan.

Lavan raced after Yaakov and his family, obviously angry and frustrated that his plan did not work. He had first tried to make Yaakov part of the gang; having failed in that, he tried to gang up on him. Lavan originally paraded as a member of the family, but he could not live with anything less than total conformity to his own devious ways. He was frustrated in his attempt to undermine and destroy Yaakov, primarily by Yaakov's strong resolve and commitment and by the total support of Lavan's daughters, Raḥel and Leah, for Yaakov.

We are grateful for the bounty of Israel. We realize that this physical bounty is directly related to the tenacity of faith of our ancestors, who in spite of all the imposed difficulties, refused to capitulate their moral values. Through the thanksgiving formula, the one who brings the first fruits realizes that any physical blessing that accrues in Israel is directly related to the spiritual prowess of Israel—the patriarch Yaakov and his family. The eating of the first fruits in Jerusalem is thus not a mere picnic outing; it is a spiritual experience. Living in Israel, and enjoying Israel, is ultimately a triumph of the spirit.

SIDRAH NIZAVIM
Down to Earth

Mosheh Rabbenu, in the last days of his leadership, shared with the people a glimpse into the future. Part of that glimpse relates to the ingathering of the exiles, the return of the captives and their gathering together.

Mosheh Rabbenu tells the people that "Even if one of your banished ones be at the ends of the heavens, from there the Lord (God) your God will gather you together and from there will take you" (Devarim 30:4). The "banished ones" (*nidahim*), the ones banished the greatest distance, they too will be part of this great ingathering.

Mosheh Rabbenu speaks of these banished ones as being far away, at the "ends of the heavens." The terminology appears to be problematic. Why is the phrase "the ends of the *heavens*" rather than "the ends of the *earth*"? What is the meaning of being banished to "the ends of the heavens"?

It may be conjectured that this refers to those who are not satisfied with life on earth and therefore seek a means of escape from this world. In past generations, the escape was probably effected through alcohol, through the high that may be achieved in a drunken state. In our generation, new ingredients have been added to the list of substances used to escape: drugs are available as a means of attaining a high in order to flee from unwelcome reality.

Mosheh Rabbenu, in this passage, is therefore addressing the matter of those who are disenchanted with life, with the community, with the world. Even those individuals will eventually be part of the ingathering. Even those who are at the ends of the heavens, seeking a high that is literally "sky high," will be brought down to earth.

The coming down to earth will be effected through God gathering you together, "and from there will take you." All those individuals who seek the highs will be gathered together in a unique meeting. They will have the opportunity to share with one another their reasons for wanting to escape, the nature of their escape, and what they gained from the attempt.

The hope, expressed in the statement of Mosheh Rabbenu, is that in this unique confrontation, they will realize the folly of their ways, that escape was a futile exercise, and that the way to live is to affirm this world and all the opportunity afforded by it. Once that is realized, from *there* God will take you. From there, from the awakening to the sacred reality of life, these individuals will be reintegrated into society and will find fulfillment in that society. Mosheh Rabbenu here gives our generation the hope that those who for whatever reason are running away will eventually realize that it is no escape from the world and, more importantly, that there is no need to escape from the world.

SIDRAH VA-YELEKH
The Unity Legacy

One of the last commandments, in fact the next to the last commandment transmitted by Mosheh Rabbenu to the Israelite community, was the mitzvah of *hakhel*. This mitzvah was the obligation to gather once every seven years, after the end of the sabbatical year, on the festival of Sukkot, for the reading of various key sections of the Torah. All the people—men, women, and children of all ages—were to gather for this majestic recreation of revelation (Devarim 31:10-13).

The legislation is introduced with the words "And Mosheh commanded them, saying . . ." (Devarim 31:10). Mosheh was speaking, as he frequently did, to the *kohanim*, but the language of the passage is unprecedented. Normally, God commands and Mosheh transmits that command to the people. Here however, the Torah portrays Mosheh as the commander: "And Mosheh commanded them . . ."

The gathering of the people, as previously indicated, took place in the aftermath of the sabbatical year. In this year, all debts were abrogated and all individuals had equal access to the fields of Israel. The sabbatical year was verily a time when the community felt a sense of oneness. No one was at a greater advantage than any one else, and all shared. The sabbatical year was the great equalizer. The people came together at the conclusion of the sabbatical year, obviously in a spirit of unity.

The poor appreciated the gestures of the wealthy and could stand side-by-side with them without feeling embarrassed or disadvantaged.

Seeing that the *hakhel* experience is intimately linked to the sabbatical year, it probably would make more sense that the mitzvah of *hakhel* should be introduced in the same legislation that established the sabbatical year. The legislation concerning the sabbatical year appears much earlier (Va-yikra 25:1-7, and further). Why, indeed, was the *hakhel* legislation not introduced at that time?

Mosheh Rabbenu, upon hearing from God about this mitzvah, may have asked God to allow him to postpone transmitting it. Mosheh Rabbenu was concerned for the unity of the Jewish people; he therefore may have interceded with God to postpone the announcement of the *hakhel* mitzvah for a more propitious moment. That moment would be just before his departure from this world. By announcing the concern for communal unity at the very end, Mosheh hoped to impress the people with the importance of unity, and that this would remain with them as an everlasting legacy.

It is perhaps for this reason that the Torah employs the words "And Mosheh commanded them . . . " The essence of the command came from God, but the timing of it came from Mosheh Rabbenu, with God's approval.

Mosheh Rabbenu insists that even though individuals live in different locations and probably do not see each other from year to year, nevertheless they must all come together at least once in seven years to listen to what makes them unique, what binds them together. The king would read to the people the fundamental affirmations of Jewish life that give the community its uniqueness and purpose. Everyone would hear the same message, and all would be obliged to adhere to that message. Thus would be reinforced the unity of purpose, in the atmosphere of the unified presence of all Israel.

Abravanel sees the majestic conclusion of the Torah every year on Simḥat Torah as a derivative expression of the *hakhel* gathering. The leader of the community concludes the Torah in the presence of the adults and children of that community. It would be ever so valuable if the community saw Simḥat Torah as a time to relive the unity expressed in the mitzvah of *hakhel*, the timing for which reflected Mosheh Rabbenu's passionate concern for the unity of Israel.

SIDRAH HA'AZINU
The Old and the New

The parting song of Mosheh Rabbenu is a combination of past and future. Mosheh Rabbenu points to past events, to the vicissitudes of Israelite history, and to a future which he hopes will reflect that the lessons of the past were not lost. Unfortunately, the contemporary realism of the song indicates that the lessons were not well learned.

One of the more devastating indictments of Mosheh Rabbenu is that the people had forgotten the Rock who brought them into the world (Devarim 32:18). This is a condemnation of the ingratitude of the people, of their turning their backs on God, who is responsible for their existence.

However, it seems evident, and Mosheh Rabbenu realizes this, that such ingratitude comes as the culmination of a syndrome. That syndrome is referred to in the preceding verse (32:17), in which Mosheh Rabbenu speaks of the people sacrificing to strange gods, "new gods that came up of late . . . "

Mosheh Rabbenu understands that the rejection of God does not come suddenly; it is the end result of a process. The process is ushered along by the penchant for newness. The people will adopt as their deity the gods that were unknown to their own parents. Through adoption of the new, they will reject the old. Their being disenchanted with life will lead to their souring on the old. One may, of course, see in this the harbinger of that great historical cleavage which unfolded approximately two thousand years ago.

The syndrome that Mosheh Rabbenu herein laments is not foreign to this generation. This is a generation, as in the pattern referred to in the aforementioned verse, which rushes to espouse the new. A new recipe, a new product, a new miracle drug, a new theory of approach to a difficult situation, all of these are exciting. A new car, a new home, a new wardrobe, these are all the objects of desire. Our generation may not worship a new god, but they certainly worship the god of newness.

Some even make the claim that it is the obligation of religion to change with the times; to be with it, to be as new as the unfolding realities. Unfortunately, the desire to embrace that which is new perforce leaves no room for that which has stood the test of time. Mosheh Rabbenu affirms that the key element in Israel's survival and continued growth is its capacity to build on the past, and to strengthen its future through its ties with the past.

The present generation often seeks to divorce itself from its parents, who are considered to be "from the older generation" and who are, by definition, out of touch. Companies feel constrained to create new products, rather than rely on those already in production. The feeling prevails that to attract the public and capture its fancy, we must offer something new and exciting. The new itself eventually becomes old and must be replaced. Nothing is sacred; everything is transitory.

Mosheh Rabbenu asks the people to "Remember the days of old, comprehend the years of the generations; ask your father and he will relate it to you, your elders and they will explain it to you" (Devarim 32:7). Mosheh Rabbenu begs the people not to go running after the exciting and the new but rather to steep themselves in tradition. He asks that they consult with the parents and the elders to learn what went on in previous generations, to learn from the mistakes of the past and not to repeat them in the future.

That which is new should be looked upon with suspicion; that which is old and has stood the test of time should be looked upon with veneration. This is the way a community of tradition evolves. This is the way the solidarity of the Jewish people can be maintained.

SIDRAH VE-ZOT HA-BERAKHAH
Uplifting Torah

The final portion of the Torah, Ve-zot Ha-Berakhah, is read on the festive occasion of Simḥat Torah. Simḥat Torah celebrates the conclusion of the cycle of reading the Torah and the beginning of the cycle anew. There is a custom among many to do a reverse lifting of the Torah on Simḥat Torah night and Simḥat Torah morning. By reversing the hands, the Torah, when it is picked up, actually points outward toward the congregation. Taamay HaMinhagim (no. 833) cites the view that this custom is linked to a statement in "Chapters of the Elders" (Pirkay Avot), "Turn it (*hafokh*) and turn it for everything is in it" (5:26). In other words, we show the Torah in a more dynamic projection. Through the Torah being turned, through the lifting being reversed (*hafokh*), we remind the congregation of how essential the Torah is for the community, that everything is in it.

Normally, when the Torah is lifted, one of the sentences recited by the congregation is "And this is the law which Mosheh set before the children of Israel" (Devarim 4:44).

This verse is found in an odd place. It is in the midst of a discussion of the setting up of cities of refuge, to which those who have killed accidently must flee (Devarim 4:41-49).

The seemingly incongruous interjection of this verse in a discussion of the cities of refuge presses home a very critical point. The Torah, as guide for life, can unfortunately also be abused. The abuse of Torah can have devastating consequences,

130 / *More Torah Therapy*

leading to irresponsible behavior, even behavior that would demand going into a city of refuge for killing accidentally.

The Talmud actually derives from this verse the observation that if a person is meritorious, the Torah becomes for that person a potion of life. However, if the person is not meritorious, the Torah can be a deadly potion (Yoma 72b). One can surmise that the Talmud too was bothered by the positioning of this passage in the midst of a discussion about cities of refuge. It derives the critical lesson that if the Torah is abused, misinterpreted, and manipulated, it can have a strong negative impact on the individual and on the community.

The custom of reciting this verse when the Torah is lifted is probably intended to shake the congregation out of any complacency. They should not think that merely because they attend services, and have just listened to the Torah, that they are guaranteed to live an exalted life. The Torah can inspire, but it can also be distorted. We are forced to realize, through the very verse that is recited, the full extent of the consequences of perverting the meaning of the Torah.

The second half of the formula recited when the Torah is lifted is "According to God's orders did they encamp and according to God's orders did they journey forth, the charge of God they did keep, according to God's order through Mosheh" (Be-midbar 9:23). Most people just add the last words of this verse, "according to God's order through Mosheh." The feeling of some is that this is erroneous, that the entire verse should be recited, since one is not permitted to splice a passage in the Torah (Berakhot 12b).

If the first verse points to the dangers of abuse of the Torah, the second verse deals with the antidote to abuse. The verse speaks about the travels of the Israelite community, and their collectively encamping and journeying forth according to God's command. The people were united and fully synchronized in their departures and arrivals. This was achieved through their all marching to God's orders. They all had the same Commander, and they all followed the same orders. They fused into a coherent, integrated, and interdependent community.

Abuse of Torah is usually related to individuals stepping out on their own, justifying their own deviation through misinterpretation, and then treating others irresponsibly. However, when communal coherence is maintained, and everyone is subordinate to the greater good of the community, then the irresponsibilities which may lead to accidental death and fleeing to cities of refuge are not likely to evolve.

When the Torah is raised, we recite a verse of admonition and a verse of advice. The first verse warns us of what can happen; the second tells us what we must do to make sure that it does not happen. By reciting these verses we try to assure that the lifting up of the Torah will be, for the community, an uplifting experience.

ROSH HASHANAH
Water, Water, Everywhere . . .

Interspersed among the more dominant themes of the Torah reading for the first day of Rosh HaShanah is a somewhat digressive story involving Hagar and her son, Yishmael. Coming after the birth of Yizḥak and the ensuing dramatic encounter between Avraham and Sarah but prior to the pact entered into between Avraham and Avimelekh, this story tends to recede into relative insignificance. But it should not, because it is not insignificant.

The story, briefly, is as follows: Avraham provides provisions for Hagar and Yishmael and reluctantly sends them on their way. After the water from the bottle was consumed, Hagar casts her son Yishmael under one of the shrubs. She sits down far away, a bowshot's distance, saying, "Let me not look upon the death of the child."

Hagar is startled by an angelic voice that interrupts her weeping. The angel asks Hagar, "*Mah lakh Hagar?*" What is with you, or more appropriately, what is the matter with you? God had heard the voice of the child crying, and the angel intervened to forestall the impending tragedy. The angel tells Hagar to get up, take the child, and hold him tight. God then "opens" Hagar's eyes and she sees a well of water. Hagar goes, refills the empty bottle, and gives her child the drink (Bereshit 21:14-19).

Hagar was not a bad mother. She obviously cared for her child. But the caring was not a mature type. She was willing and able to care for the child as long as all went well. But the onset of a crisis brought great difficulties for her. Instead of trying her best to attempt a solution to her dilemma, she gave up almost immediately. And then, instead of staying with her child through the agony of his dying from lack of water, she left him alone to die, because she could not take the pain.

We cannot but feel for Hagar's pain, but there is something wrong. The fact that you distance yourself from someone else's pain does not mean that the pain is gone. That is an illusion. Worse than that, that very pain is exacerbated by the thought that no one cares. Others may care very much about the pain, but not so much that they are willing to share it, and thereby alleviate it somewhat. If we do not care that much about others' pain, by what justification do we come to God on Rosh HaShanah and ask that God take cognizance of our pain?

The angel asks Hagar, What is the matter with you? In effect, the angel is asking Hagar what kind of a mother she purports to be? A true mother never abandons her child, nor does a father abandon his child. Any agony felt by the child is somewhat relieved by the fact that he or she is not alone.

Being a parent is not a joy ride, any more than being part of life is a joy ride. There are always challenges and difficulties, minor or major, that must be confronted. Those who withdraw at the smallest challenge may salve themselves with the thought that they have avoided some pain, but what they have really done is to avoid life itself.

There is no life without pain, and no growth without overcoming some challenge or obstacle. The shofar sounds of Rosh HaShanah are *tear*ing sounds. They are tears that tear away at us, awakening us to the imperatives that we must face, if we are to have a life of meaning.

There is light at the end of the struggle. God opens up Hagar's eyes and she sees a well of water. Was this a miracle, a new well appearing from nowhere? Hardly. Sforno states that the well was there, but the will to find it was not. God opened her eyes to what was already there, but which Hagar failed to see, because she had closed her eyes and shut herself off from the challenge.

This was, for Hagar and for us, an eye-opening experience. So often in life, when we are faced with great burdens, we blame others, or circumstances, for our travail. But so often the problem is not out there, and the solution is right here, within us. Not always, but often enough.

We hear the advice that we should stay within ourselves, rather than doing too much or trying too hard. But this also means that we should not try to do too little. It is within ourselves to cope with pain, to channel our energies properly in a moment of crisis, to buckle up and forcefully confront a crisis, and thereby increase our chances of overcoming it. Once we realize this, we will, as did Hagar, take those available resources, and fill up our bottle with them.

As parents, we might try to look the other way as our children behave in a less than constructive, even destructive way. But staying a bowshot's distance from the child solves nothing. It is reckless abandonment.

The child who is withering away is crying for life, and needs someone who really cares; it needs a parent. We dare not create distance when closeness is needed. We dare not shut our eyes when our eyes should be opened wide to what is unfolding. Yes, this is more painful, but only for the moment. Ask any parent whose caring intervention saved a child whether it was worth the effort and pain; the answer is invariably in the affirmative.

Thus, the message of the Hagar story is twofold: we can do it, and since we can do it, we must do it. For, by caring and sharing, we lighten the pain of others. And what we do for others, family or friends, others will do for us. Including, hopefully, the ultimate other, God.

ROSH HASHANAH
The *Akedah* — A Test within a Test

The *Akedah*, the story of the binding of Isaac, is at once a daily staple and a Rosh HaShanah highlight. It is a daily staple in that it is a part of the regular daily prayer liturgy, and it is a Rosh HaShanah highlight in that it is one of the two Torah readings for Rosh HaShanah.

We tend to consider the *Akedah* as a test of Avraham's faith. Would Avraham agree to a request from God that went against logic and reason and seemed to contradict basic human and theological principles?

It is possible that there is another dimension to the test, one that may be the primary one. This possibility is that the *Akedah* was not only a test of Avraham's belief but also a test of Avraham's parenting. The real challenge to Avraham was whether he could convince Yizḥak to go along with him.

By approaching Avraham, God left Avraham with a possible escape hatch. He could have come back to God and said that he approached Yizḥak with the proposition of being given back to God, but that Yizḥak was not so eager and that therefore it may not be such a good idea. The test here was twofold. Firstly, did Avraham's faith allow him to carry through God's request, and secondly, would he be able to convince his son Yizḥak to go along?

For Yizḥak to be willing to go along, two basic ingredients were required; Avraham's eagerness and a solid parent-child relationship between Avraham and Yizḥak. With regard to Avraham's eagerness, it is self-evident that if Avraham would have approached the situation half-heartedly, he surely could not have expected to inspire Yizḥak to go along. With regard to the parent-child relationship, if Avraham and Yizḥak had developed a mutual trust over the course of their years together, then Avraham could have asked of Yizḥak almost anything, and Yizḥak would have been sure to go along. Whether Yizḥak would go along would reflect retroactively on the type of parent that Avraham was. Was Avraham an indulging parent who catered to every whim of his child? Or was Avraham the type of parent who elicited from his child the faith and transcending commitment that knew no bounds?

Twice in the *Akedah* we are told that both of them, Avraham and Yizḥak, walked together (Bereshit 22:6, 8). One can see this as an emphasis on the togetherness that prevailed between father and son, and reflected well on the relationship; a relationship of trust that was so strong that even when Avraham came to Yizḥak with this outlandish request, Yizḥak readily went along.

The *Akedah* story is a daily staple and a Rosh HaShanah highlight. It is a staple, because it addresses not only the notion of faith, but also the importance of parent-child trust. This trust only develops through the day-by-day commitment. It is at the same time a highlight, because it is so vital to Jewish continuity. How the parent raises the child and how the child then behaves toward the parent are crucial for the cementing of transgenerational ties.

I recently read of a famous football coach who is well known for his recruiting strategy, which is so important in the building of strong football teams. This college coach once went quite a distance, about three hundred miles, to interview a much heralded prospect. However, about five minutes into the interview, which the coach, as was his habit, conducted in the player's home, the coach heard the prospect say to his mother, "Shut up!" The coach instantly got up and left. If a person did not have proper respect for parents, the coach did not want that person on his football team. What applies to football, applies even more significantly in life. The *Akedah* stands out as that experience in which the respect of child for parent gained ultimate expression.

There are many ways in which we could recall the *Akedah* on Rosh HaShanah. There were a number of instruments that were involved, including an altar, a rope, and a knife. We remember the *Akedah* with none of these instruments. Instead, we remember the *Akedah* with the shofar, the ram's horn; reminiscent of the ram which was brought to the altar after Yiẓḥak was unbound. Since it was the ram rather than Yiẓḥak that was sacrificed, the shofar symbolizes the notion that God ultimately did not desire that the child be given back; God desired that the child live.

The experience of the *Akedah* projected for all generations the extent of the profound love and respect that should prevail between parent and child. The ultimate message of the *Akedah* is that God wants the child to live and to be a vibrant part of Jewish continuity. The challenge on Rosh HaShanah is for us to make sure that this unfolds in our own environment.

YOM KIPPUR
Guilt Trip—Worthwhile Journey

On Yom Kippur, we come face-to-face with an ugly word, guilt. The more we hear about the negative components of guilt, and that it is best avoided, the more it continues to surface as an ubiquitous reality of human life. The problem is not really with the guilt per se, which is a neutral component of life. The problem is how we deal with guilt. We are all guilty in one way or another, whether it be for what we have done or for what we should have done. If we wallow in the guilt, we are in trouble. If we grow because of it, we are involved in a dynamic human endeavor.

The ideal approach to guilt is based on an insightful comment in the Talmud concerning the individual who repents out of joy, out of love. This repentance transmutes the previous breaches into positive fulfillments (Yoma 86b).

The behavior dynamic suggested in this Talmudic statement is quite instructive. An individual who confronts a previous action and realizes that such action was contemptible, and who honestly and soberly assesses that action, using the breach as a springboard to a more positive approach, has in fact transmuted that sin into a fulfillment. The sin has been used as an instrument for future positive behavior.

At times, individuals who perform a good deed may be so impressed with themselves because of that good deed that they are likely to absolve themselves of many future responsibilities. In such a reaction, the commandment is invested with a negative energy. On the other hand, one can invest a transgression with a positive energy.

The Day of Atonement, the day on which the community as a whole and all individuals within the community are expected to confront their sins, is known as Yom Kippur. Interestingly, the word "*kippur*," although usually translated as atonement, is more closely linked with the Hebrew word for covering over, not in the sense of hiding something, but in the sense of overlaying, covering the basic material (Bereshit 6:14).

The implication of this is that on the Day of Atonement we do not make past breaches disappear, because what has happened cannot be erased. Rather, we can build upon the past, however contemptible, and overlay it with good deeds that in fact smother the sin and transmute the sin into a fulfillment. In a word, one may glorify life by rising above circumstances; one may learn from the past to build for the future.

In other words, the Talmud suggests, instead of wallowing in the self-pity that comes with suffering "guilt from," it is preferable to think along the lines of "guilt toward," of pointing the guilt to the future, and using it as a directional compass to indicate where one should go in the future.

This general approach is useful for individuals who are dealing with their own specific guilt-ridden circumstances. It may even be a good underpinning for the clinical approach to guilt on a cognitive level.

It may be more preferable, in confronting the guilt of a woman who feels badly about having had an abortion performed for nonmedical reasons, to look for ways to learn from the guilt feeling in a positive manner. This may take the form of adopting a child or of becoming pregnant once again and carrying through to term.

The individual who feels guilty about not having done enough for a parent or another loved one who has just passed away may have legitimate reasons for feeling this way. An approach that would try to absolve the individual from this guilt feeling may sometimes be less appropriate than suggesting that the guilt may be legitimate, but that what is past is past and cannot be brought back. Confronting the reality of deficiencies in one's past behavior, one can therefore be urged to go an extra mile with a surviving parent or other loved ones. In other words, the approach orients toward the future, rather than explicating the past.

Guilt, far from being a negative component of life, can be the spark which gives life meaning. We have a *right* to be guilty and a responsibility to confront that guilt. Taking a guilt trip with a future focus may be the most worthwhile voyage of life.

YOM KIPPUR
Collective Guilt

Viktor Frankl relates the story of a woman who complained to him about the fact that he wrote in the German language. She questioned how he could do this after all the evil perpetrated by the Germans. Frankl asked the woman if she had any knives in her kitchen. When the lady said yes, Frankl asked how she could use knives when she realized how many people have been killed by knives. The lady stopped bothering him about his use of German.

Obviously, the matter of collective guilt goes beyond this exchange. Frankl was venturing a view with regard to blaming individuals for the actions of others simply because they are from the same nationality or the same ethnic origin. The matter of collective guilt is perhaps best understood within the context of collective responsibility. Hannah Arendt addresses this matter quite eloquently. She asserts that we are not speaking about imposing a collective guilt upon a specific group of individuals.

> In political terms, the idea of humanity, excluding no people and assigning a monopoly of guilt to no one, is the only guarantee that one "superior race" after another may not feel obligated to follow the "natural law" of the right of the powerful, and exterminate "inferior races unworthy of survival"; so that at the end of an "imperialistic age" we should find ourselves in a stage which would

make the Nazis look like crude precursors of future political method. (Arendt, in R. Smith, *Guilt: Man and Society*, 1971, p. 267)

Arendt goes on to praise the Judaic approach, in that it incorporated the idea of collective guilt as collective responsibility for humankind through the liturgical formula recited each year, "Our Father and King, we have sinned before you" (ibid.). What Arendt did not realize is that this concept is not expressed merely once a year (on Yom Kippur) but is found in the regular prayers recited thrice daily; it appears in the *Amidah*. We ask God to pardon us for we have sinned (*s'laḥ lanu . . . ki ḥatanu*).

In what way have we sinned? It would make sense if the statement read "forgive me because I have sinned" or "pardon me because I have sinned," but why "pardon *us*"? The answer, as Arendt herself suggests for Yom Kippur, is that collective responsibility is a matter that is so crucial that recognition of it is not limited to one time a year. It is imprinted upon our consciousness three times a day. Even if an individual may not be directly responsible for the actions of others, there is a collective responsibility. There is always a possibility that our intervention or help may have precluded the commission of a crime.

Arendt thinks that no individual should be content with the hypocritical confession that "God be thanked, I am not like that" (ibid.), in reaction to the evil perpetrated by the Nazis and others.

> Rather, in fear and trembling, have they finally realized of what man is capable—and this is indeed the precondition of any modern political thinking. Such persons will not serve very well as functionaries of vengeance. This, however, is certain: upon them and only upon them, who are filled with a genuine fear of the inescapable guilt of the human race, can there be any reliance when it comes to

fighting fearlessly, uncompromisingly, everywhere against the incalculable evil that men are capable of bringing about. (ibid.)

The point made by Arendt is quite clear. It is also noteworthy that the emphasis is on collective guilt in the positive preventive sense, as an alarm to warn against a future massive calamity.

On Yom Kippur, we confront ourselves as individuals and as part of a collective, part of a community. Through the *Ashamnu* ("We have sinned") and the *Al Ḥet* pronouncements, both stated in the collective sense, we elicit our sense of communal responsibility. We culminate the year-round, daily expression of that responsibility with a more detailed elaboration on that theme. To the extent that we focus on the personal and communal future through a profound appreciation of the personal and communal past, of our actions and inactions, to that extent will we be able, collectively, to make Yom Kippur a day of surpassing significance.

PESAH
What If?

What if? If things had been different, how would the world look now? This is a question that at first blush merely feeds one's curiosity for the hypothetical, and nothing more. What if Columbus had not discovered America? What if the United States had lost the War of 1812? What if the State of Israel had not been reestablished in 1948? What if Mikhail Gorbachev had not become the leader of the former Soviet Union? Since all these events did actually take place, it appears to be a waste of time to ask, "What if?" But there are "what ifs" that are more than mere curiosity, "what ifs" that project important messages about who we are.

One such "what if" deals with the enslavement of the Israelites in Egypt, the cruel bondage and the miraculous redemption. What if that had not occurred? What if the Israelites had never ventured into Egypt, and had never become enslaved? Surely, much that has become basic Judaic affirmation would not have attained that status. Our daily liturgy of thanksgiving to God for the Exodus would be missing. There would be no mention of this great event in the Shema, the Ten Commandments, the Kiddush, among other places. And, needless to say, we would have no Passover to celebrate.

In a convoluted way, this argument from the hypothetical almost leads to the proposition that we should be grateful to the ancient Egyptians for the legacy bequeathed by their cruelty. This is hardly a pleasant thought. It is likewise inconsistent with our expressed revulsion at the evil perpetrated by Israel's taskmasters.

But what about the "what if"? It seems that, no matter how, the Israelites were destined to be enslaved. God, in that famous covenantal encounter with Avraham, then still Avram, tells him that his posterity will be enslaved in a foreign land, after which they will experience a great redemption (Bereshit 15:13-14). That Israel would be enslaved was already a foregone conclusion long before the event itself, and prior to any acts of insubordination or rebellion that may have preceded the exile and servitude.

Avraham, that great defender of justice, does not utter a murmur of protest at the news that his posterity will suffer. He does not ask why; he accepts it. There is great promise for Israel, but that promise comes at a price. That price is the enslavement of the community of Israel, an enslavement that would unfold prior to Israel being redeemed and taken unto God as the people who would live by God's word.

To paraphrase a famous statement of Jean Paul Sartre, had there been no Egypt, we would have had to invent it! Why? The reason for this relates to the essence of the Torah. The Torah is founded on the profound relationship between God and Israel. The Torah itself contains so many regulations that relate to the area of human sensitivity. We are obliged to love the stranger, since we were strangers in the land of Egypt (Devarim 10:19). We are obliged to be sensitive to the Egyptians, since they gave us domicile in their land (Devarim 23:8).

There is an entire complement of laws adjuring our empathy for the poor and delicacy in human relations. Is it humanly possible for a people to keep up with such laws? Is it possible for mortals, with a natural proclivity for creature comfort, to actually behave in a self-transcending way? It is possible, yet not necessarily likely.

But our enslavement prior to attaining nationhood changed all that. The people as a collective whole lived through the firsthand experience of deprivation; wives living widowlike as single parents, husbands separated from their families and living in physical impoverishment, children cruelly manhandled and denied the basic pleasures of being parented in a joyous manner.

The Israelites were given a never-to-be-forgotten lesson in the elementary needs that all humans have, but which very few appreciate. Having suffered through the verbal abuse, they could better appreciate what a heinous crime it is to speak callously. Having lived through separation and poverty, they could better appreciate the plight of the poor and the orphan, and could thus better fulfill the Torah requirements toward these unfortunates. We did not, however, need the excessive cruelty of the Egyptians, the murder and inhumane punishment. In this cruelty they acted as independent agents, not as agents of God's purpose.

Had our early history been filled with uninterrupted happiness and prosperity, we likely would never have aspired to abide by God's word. As it is, the challenge is great, but our early history gave us some hope that we would be up to the challenge.

So, on Pesah, we celebrate our freedom, a freedom we could not really appreciate without it first having been denied us. We never complain about the antecedent enslavement. We realize that this is part of our history, and that this enslavement has made it possible for us to fine-tune our human sensitivity.

The answer to the question "What if?" is clear. No matter what, servitude would have preceded nationhood; otherwise, our nationhood would have been nothing more than mass narcissism.

On Pesah, we express our gratitude to God for the redemption, and our appreciation to our ancestors for having endured, and for having transmitted to us the legacy and human qualities that make fulfillment of Judaic responsibility a legitimate possibility.

PESAḤ
Questions and the Questioner

The dialogue of the Pesaḥ seder is launched by the recitation of "*Mah Nishtanah* . . . ?," a series of four questions which are directed to the parents by the children and which are intended to elicit a response from the parents. Education is not best achieved by monologue; it is best achieved through dialogue. Teachers may ramble on and get the information and ideas out of their systems, but it is unclear whether these ideas enter into the minds and hearts of the students. A dialogue with the students enables the teacher to determine whether the lesson has been effective.

On Pesaḥ night we cannot take chances. To ensure that the reading of the Haggadah is not merely the reading of words by the leader of the seder, it is imperative that the children ask questions. The reading of the Haggadah then becomes not a monologue but part of a dialogue; it becomes a response to the child's questions. The spirit of the Haggadah dictates that not only must the answer be given, it must also be understood and appreciated by the questioning children.

The Four Questions are planted questions; they are not original, but standard. The questions are mere prompts to begin a dialogue. The leader's response that is provided in the Haggadah is really nothing more than a bare-bones framework, with ample room to fill in nuances of significance.

The questions address four essential characteristics that make the seder unique. They thus open up avenues of further inquiry about the meaning and significance of the Exodus for Jewish destiny. The questions concern (1) *matzah*, (2) *maror* (bitter herbs), (3) dipping certain foods in salt water or *haroset* and (4) eating in a reclining position. These four may be divided into two distinct categories. The first category relates to the type of food eaten—*matzah* and *maror*; the second category deals with the manner in which the food is eaten—dipping the food and eating in a reclining position.

The original call to join in the seder, "Whoever is hungry should come and eat, whoever is in need should come and celebrate Pesah," is somewhat perplexing. The invitation is extended after the fact, on the evening of Pesah itself, and it is issued in the confines of the home, unheard by anyone who may be outside. What is the meaning of this type of invitation?

It may be that this summons is directed to the household, to the members of the family. Those who are *hungry* are told that they can expect a good meal. Those who are *in need*, ostensibly in need of help and direction in understanding the meaning of Pesah and the seder, are also invited to come and celebrate together. Two invitations are thus extended, a prandial invitation and a spiritual invitation. The leader of the seder thus shows a great understanding of the children. There is little care given as to why the children will join, as long as they will join. Once they are there, it becomes the obligation of the leader to make sure that the seder experience is a meaningful one.

The questions that are asked in the *Mah Nishtanah* relate to the prandial and spiritual invitations. For the prandial invitation, the questions relating to the type of food, namely *matzah* and *maror*, seem particularly relevant. For the spiritual invitation, the questions relating to change in style and manner seem to be more pertinent. They are questions which seek to explore the reasons for changes not so much in what we eat but in how we eat.

For each of the two categories, the prandial and the spiritual, there are two questions. The two questions indicate two departures in each dimension. One departure could probably be explained without the necessity of a full contemplation on the unique nature of the seder. Two departures, however, are reason to pause and reflect.

Parenthetically, this approach clarifies somewhat why the aforementioned questions were chosen to launch the retrospective evening of the seder. It also explains why drinking four cups of wine was not the subject of one of the questions. The four cups reflect neither a change of menu nor of manner, except insofar as they are consumed in a reclining position, a change already asked about in the last of the Four Questions. The four cups point only to a change in quantity. Although requiring the consumption of four cups of wine may be significant, it is pedagogically not as significant a change from the usual as are the other changes noted in the Four Questions.

The questions have been asked, but the questioners may differ. The Haggadah notes that there are four different types of children who may ask the questions. The leader of the seder is urged to be aware of who is asking the questions. The response must be appropriate not only to the question but also to the questioner. The object of the seder evening is not for the leader to show brilliance or impressive mastery of the text; it is for the leader to assure the interest of the child or children, to maintain lines of communication, and to link the generations. The ultimate purpose of the seder is to develop and establish in the children a faith in God so that they orient their daily lives around God's word—the Torah.

The seder structure is thus set up to make possible an uplifting learning experience. If the Haggadah is the bare bones, it is up to each and every one to put flesh onto those bones and life into the next generation.

SHAVUOT
A Fair Hearing

The Torah describes the awesome nature of *Mattan Torah* (the giving of the Torah) with a peculiar phrase: "And all the people saw the sounds . . . " (Shemot 20:15). Rashi notes the apparent confusion of the senses in this phrase: "They saw that which should be heard, something which is impossible to see on any other occasion."

In our media-oriented society, people's opinions are formulated in direct proportion to the coverage given events and issues. Will Rogers's famous statement "All I know is what I see in the papers" may now be extended to include television, radio, and magazines. One might also say that we judge by our ears, by the decibel count of the news, rather than by qualitative judgments.

The Talmud (Berakhot 58a) illustrates the ultimate in sense perception in the story of Rav Sheshet, a blind sage who showed better vision than a contemporary with healthy eyes.

> Rav Sheshet was blind, yet, when the whole community once went out to meet the king, he went out with them, and was met by a certain heretic who laughed at him saying: "All the earthen pitchers are indeed going to the stream [to draw water]; whither do the broken vessels go?" "Come!" Rav Sheshet said unto him, "I will show you that I know more than you do." When the first company of troops passed by making a great noise, the heretic

asked, "Has the king passed?" "No," replied Rav Sheshet. When a second group of troops passed, the heretic again asked whether the king had passed. Again Rav Sheshet answered "No." A third company passed in a very quiet manner. The heretic asked: "Is the king coming now?" Whereupon Rav Sheshet answered, "Yes."

The Talmud continues and explains how the sage knew this, alluding to the Divine manifestation as emanating from silence. Rav Sheshet perceived that which people normally judge through their ears. He sensed that greatness is not in being heard, but in qualitative perception, *ro'eh*. On Mount Sinai, too, the awesomeness was apprehended not merely through the thunderous proclamation but through perception of the voice as a Divine emanation.

Perhaps the key difference between "hearing through understanding" and "understanding through being heard" is that the former concentrates on qualitative essences, whereas the latter satisfies itself with superficial facades. The way Israel accepted the Torah is a clear statement that it is the message, not the medium, that is crucial.

SHAVUOT
Forced to Choose

Shavuot celebrates the collective acceptance of the Torah by the Israelite community. The very nature of that acceptance remains problematic. Was it a free choice of the people, or was it a choice that was imposed upon the people? It seems clear from the Torah that the people accepted the Code of Law of their own free will. They said to God, when offered the Code, that we will actualize and we will understand (Shemot 24:7).

Not only did the people accept, they accepted unconditionally, even before they were aware of all that they were accepting. They accepted the Torah on faith, without knowing the full contents of the code to which they were binding themselves and future generations. Additionally, as if to further applaud this commitment, the Talmud reports that Israel was appropriately acknowledged and praised by God for having made such an unconditional and binding decision in faith (Shabbat 89b).

On the other hand, on the basis of the comment "and they stood by the nether part of the mount" (Shemot 19:17), the Talmud derives that God turned the mountain upon them like an inverted tub and said to Israel, "If you accept the Torah, it is well, but if not, there shall be your burial [undoing]" (Shabbat 88a). The Talmud even sees this as a built-in excuse for noncompliance with the Torah. Since the Torah was given in an atmosphere of coercion, those who do not comply can hardly be blamed. The Talmud then concludes that what was accepted

Shavuot / 153

under coercion at Mount Sinai was later accepted through free will in the time of Esther and Mordekhai.

The question remains: Did the Israelite community accept the Torah of their own free will, as seems to be indicated in the terminology of acceptance, or was the Torah imposed upon them, as suggested in the passage of the Talmud just cited?

There is a view proposed in Midrash Tanḥuma (Noaḥ 3), which attempts to strike some sort of median position, affirming both views simultaneously. The written Torah was accepted gracefully and by free will, while the oral law, which included a host of regulations and was much more difficult to maintain, was only accepted under duress.

Another way of affirming both views, rather than seeing them as opposing each other, is through a better understanding of the notion of free will. We are prone to think of free will in terms of limitless choices, of having all options set before us and then deciding from among those options.

However, sometimes too much choice is no choice at all. If there are too many options, then we are so burdened with having to properly comprehend the vastness of choice that we are too overwhelmed to choose. Freedom, in the words of a prominent modern philosopher, presupposes restrictions and is contingent upon restrictions. A freedom devoid of all restrictions would be closer to arbitrariness than to freedom. For choice to be real, the alternatives must be clearly spelled out and the issues must be quite obvious.

A clear example in this regard is the violin string. A violin string that moves about freely cannot be the source of good music. The violin string can yield music only when it is tied down tightly at both ends. Meaningful choice means being tied down to clear options.

When God turned the tub upside down and thereby established the boundaries within which the community could move, God thereby established clear alternatives for the Israelite community. The Talmud could have employed other instruments than the tub to imply coercion—perhaps a weapon. One must therefore see in the metaphor of the tub a message of its own. The metaphor of the tub projects the notion of a limited sphere within which one can travel, a sphere which is bounded on all sides. The choice for the people was clear. It was a choice of two alternatives, the one being vibrant life, which would be good for them, the other being death, the fate that awaited them if they would choose a life devoid of the ethical and moral responsibility spelled out in the Torah.

Faced with this clear choice of alternatives, the people were then able to choose. They were not given carte blanche to *pick and choose* how many of the commandments they wanted, when they wanted to observe them, and how they should observe them. They were given a package, and the alternative was Yes or No. They were *coerced into choosing.* This is the conclusion that one is led to in reconciling the apparently opposing views suggested in the Talmud. These views are thus not opposites but two components of a totality, giving a more profound understanding of the true nature of free choice.

SUKKOT
To Have ... To Be

Sukkot is a time of the year when we give much attention to beautifying our surroundings. Much effort and energy is expended in assuring that the sukkah, the abode for the duration of the festival, is appropriately decorated to reflect our proper valuation of the commandment to live in the sukkah. Many also go out of their way to purchase an *etrog* of appropriate beauty, together with the *lulav*, *hadasim*, and *aravot*.

Aside from the *etrog*, which by biblical fiat must be beautiful (Va-yikra 23:40), the imperative to invest the other items with beauty comes from a different source. That source is from a verse in Shemot (15:2), "this is my God, and I will adorn God . . . " According to the Talmud, this means that one is obliged to adorn oneself before God in the fulfillment of the precepts, by making a beautiful sukkah, by acquiring a beautiful *lulav*, a beautiful shofar, beautiful fringes, and so forth (Shabbat 133b).

In other words, this verse applies to any specific instrumentality for the fulfillment of a commandment. All these should reflect the worth that we attach to the commandment. Two of the classical ways of showing how we value the commandment are adorning the instruments in a beautiful manner and assuring the high quality of the Torah, the tefillin, the mezuzah.

In that same talmudic passage, another opinion is ventured concerning the interpretation of the biblical phrase "this is my God, and I will adorn God . . . " This is the opinion of Abba Shaul, who interprets the verse as a charge to be like God. This view involves a play on the word *v'anvayhu*, which is a combination of the words *ani* and *v'hu*, meaning I and He, referring to God and the individual, who should behave in a godly fashion. Thus, according to Abba Shaul, this phrase is an imperative that we should emulate God. Just as God is gracious and compassionate, so we should be gracious and compassionate.

Does Abba Shaul disagree with the original interpretation, which sees the verse as an obligation to adorn the precepts? It can be conjectured that Abba Shaul does not disagree with that interpretation. Rather, he is merely adding another necessary ingredient to complete the picture.

Abba Shaul may have been worried about a pattern that could develop through too great an emphasis on the imperative to adorn the precepts. While there is nothing wrong, and there is much right, with adorning the precepts, there is a danger that too much emphasis on adorning the precepts and on beautifying objects will cause one to lose sight of one's self. If all religiosity is spent on instrumentalities, and one's self is neglected, this is not an adornment of God at all. It is a disparagement of God and all that God represents.

Abba Shaul was singularly aware of this possibility. He therefore addressed himself to this question through an additional derivation from the verse. True, there is an obligation to beautify the commandments, but there is also an obligation to beautify the individual who is performing the commandment. The object should be beautiful, but the subject must likewise be beautiful. What better way is there for the individual to attain inner beauty, than to be like God in the exercise of graciousness and compassion?

The ultimate glorification of God is manifested in a pervasive beauty, an inner and outer beauty, a beauty of subject and object.

The message of Abba Shaul, which clearly should not be lost on this generation, is that as important as it is to *have* beauty, so it is likewise important to *be* beautiful to one's inner core. This is the formula through which Sukkot, and indeed all the commandments, attain their intended purpose.

SUKKOT
Religion as an Antidepressant

The picture we usually have of religious expression is one of intenseness and seriousness, even to the point of being oblivious to the external environment, in the performance of the commandments. The seriousness with which carrying out the commandments is approached often leads to worry, anxiety, and even distress about being unable to perform the commandment the way one would like.

The Talmud tells us that the Divine presence cannot be found among individuals who are depressed (Shabbat 30b). Religious expression may be associated with a certain amount of melancholy, but the Talmud clearly states that melancholy is not the ideal. The living of Judaic norms should be in an atmosphere of joy and should effectively engender an atmosphere of joy.

There is no better time to contemplate and to actually implement this imperative than the festival of Sukkot, for which the obligation to be joyous is repeated three times in the Torah. The Gaon of Vilna mentions that the obligation to experience the joy of Yom Tov is the most complicated commandment, since it means that we are not allowed to be upset, depressed, or angry, or to have any other emotion that diminishes joy.

Needless to say, observance of commandments is dependent on a certain amount of *mazal* (luck). The commandment to keep kosher has a relatively good *mazal*, and within religious circles "*glatt* kosher" has even greater *mazal*. "*Cholov Yisrael*" has *mazal*, as does the Shabbat. *Matzah shemurah* and scrupulousness about Hanukkah candles also are examples of commandments which have been blessed with good fortune.

One mitzvah which has not been blessed with good fortune is the mitzvah to be joyous on Yom Tov. If we were to interpret this mitzvah according to its intended ideal, it means that we must go out of our way to create an atmosphere of pure joy throughout the entire period of the Yom Tov. We would then not allow anything to upset us, no argument to encroach upon the celebrative atmosphere, no depressing mood to interfere with Yom Tov.

The Torah linkage of joy with religious celebration is predicated on the assumption that a depressed individual cannot be happy about the world and thus cannot be grateful to God for being placed in the world. True religious expression must be experienced in joy, in order that one's entire life outlook be a positive one, one which acknowledges, and is grateful to, God for being allowed to take part in this world.

We are living in a time of apparent resurgence of religious practice. However, all too often this resurgence is associated with material commandments, such as buying expensive *tefillin*, *matzah shemurah*, expensive *etrogim*, and so forth. This is often to the neglect of the emotive sphere of Judaism, a sphere which is emphasized quite markedly in the Torah, but which we have seemingly brushed aside as nonessential.

In the long run, however, the more Judaism is projected as a joyous celebration of life in God's world, the greater the likelihood that in these times of economic and emotional depression, Judaism will be an attractive alternative to many who have previously been alienated from their faith.

SHEMINI ATZERET-SIMḤAT TORAH
The Route to our Roots

The Shemini Atzeret-Simḥat Torah period is punctuated with the theme of *hakafot*. Literally, the term *"hakafah"* refers to going around and coming back to one's original source, or starting point. *Hakafot* are a unique mode of expression associated with Simḥat Torah, which coincides with Shemini Atzeret in Israel and is celebrated on the second day of Shemini Atzeret outside Israel.

There are many possible routes one could take with a Torah when it is taken out of the ark. The route that Jews have chosen, going from the ark, around, and back to the ark, expresses at once an historical yearning and a pedagogical lesson. Historically, the Torah emanates from Zion, from the epicenter of Jewish life in Jerusalem. The Israelite community established its theological roots and foundations in the Land of Israel, with Jerusalem as its center.

Israel's sojourn in the Land of Israel was interrupted by exile. The *hakafot* express the historical yearning that though we were making the rounds of the entire world from the moment of exile, driven from country to country and continent to continent, we will one day return to our starting point, the Land of Israel. This historical yearning has of course been fulfilled in our time.

At the same time, the roundabout route of the *hakafot* is a pedagogical lesson. In our history, we have had incidents of people returning to Judaism even though their parental traditions were atheistic or agnostic. On the other hand, individuals brought up in a religious environment have assimilated. These are exceptions to the general rule that the apple does not fall far from the tree. This means that children generally reflect the values of their parents. Even though a child may venture forth and make the rounds of the world, when that child eventually settles down, the life pattern adopted will generally approximate the life pattern originally established by the parents.

We usually ultimately return to the place we started. Life is a cycle, and the route that we take most often returns us to our starting point. With the *hakafot*, therefore, we indicate the parents' responsibility to be a living source of Torah which the child can emulate. No matter where the child may go, it is hoped that the child will come back full circle to the roots of a viable tradition established by the parent.

There is a verse in the Torah that is rooted in the notion of *hakafot*, "You shall not round the corners of your heads..." (Va-yikra 19:27). In Hebrew, the phrase "You shall not round" is "*Lo takifu.*" One can immediately see the connective link between *hakafot* and *takifu*. *Hakafah* means going around and coming back to the source. This biblical prohibition, *lo takifu*, is that we are not allowed to round the head.

Having spelled out the historical and pedagogical implications of going around, it would seem logical that we should recommend rounding the head as a Judaic norm. Instead, the Torah specifically prohibits rounding. It obligates us to have sideburns that straddle the ear. Why?

The reasoning behind the biblical prohibition inheres in the idea that the human being must essentially step beyond the self. This means going beyond self-expression and moving toward exemplifying the values and norms of the Torah in one's life. We take the Torah with us wherever we go, but where we go and what we do goes beyond self-expression.

Individuals who round the top of their head symbolically state that all revolves around themselves. The individual is the entire circle—the starting point, the routing, and the end point.

However, what may be true about the direction we take in life, in that we go from the source and back to the source, does not apply to ourselves as individuals. We do not revolve around ourselves; we should not concern ourselves only with personal matters. We are obliged as human beings to transcend ourselves and to embrace other individuals and other causes and values. The Torah projects this through the prohibition of rounding the head. There must be points of emanation from the roundness, sideburns which indicate a stepping outside of the self and toward the value world. The sideburns essentially emanate from the head, or from the brain, and point toward the heart. They indicate a direction toward the values of kindness, empathy, and concern that are basic Torah.

Therefore, we do not make a *hakafah* around our head. Rather, we use our head to go beyond ourselves. In life, however, we symbolize, through the *hakafot*, that where we come from, the root source of all our values, is vital. No matter where we go and however we transcend ourselves, we should be anchored in and directed toward those selfsame values.

ZAKHOR AND PARAH
Remembering what we would like to Forget

The month of Adar is punctuated with a number of special Shabbatot. The Shabbat immediately prior to or coinciding with Rosh Ḥodesh Adar is Shabbat Shekalim. The Shabbat immediately prior to Purim is Shabbat Zakhor, and the Shabbat toward the end of Adar is Shabbat Parah. At the very end of Adar or the very beginning of Nisan is Shabbat HaḤodesh, on which Shabbat the Torah reading begins to set the mood for Pesaḥ, since it contains the first and basic directives for Pesaḥ preparation.

Shabbat Shekalim anticipates the giving of the *shekalim* at Purim. It is a reminder of the fact that at this time the announcement for the giving of *shekalim* was made (Mishnah Shekalim 1:1).

The observance of Shabbat Zakhor is obviously related to Purim, in that we are asked through Zakhor to remember Amalek, and to renew our commitment to eliminate the vestiges of Amalek, that is, the practice of wanton hatred, from our midst. The connection between Amalek and Purim is immediately obvious, since Haman, the archvillain of Purim, was a descendant of Amalek.

The story of Purim and the existence of hatred even today are stark reminders that the hatred of the past is not mere history; it is recurring history.

What is less clear is the reasoning for the reading of the laws concerning the red heifer, the *parah adumah*, on Shabbat Parah.

This Shabbat, as mentioned previously, occurs toward the end of the month of Adar. According to some, the obligation to read this legislation is a biblical obligation, much as the obligation to read of our responsibility to eliminate the vestiges of Amalek is a biblical obligation (Shulḥan Arukh, Oraḥ Ḥayyim 685:7).

Since, in the absence of the *Bet HaMikdash*, the red heifer is a ritual which does not apply in the present generation, one wonders why we must remember this on a regular basis.

One may conjecture that this is in order to keep in the forefront of our minds the primacy of the *Bet HaMikdash* and our yearning for its restoration. However, this could be effected through other readings, including those dealing with other rituals associated with the *Bet HaMikdash*. Why specifically the red heifer?

Rabbi Barukh Epstein (*Torah Temimah*, Be-midbar 19:21, note 125) suggests that we read the regulations of the red heifer not for their own sake, but because of a related matter. Rashi (Be-midbar 19:22), indicates that the red heifer was intended to atone for the worshiping of the golden calf. The golden calf calamity involved the worship of a sacred cow—something which had material value and was deified. We take a red heifer—letter-perfect and without blemish—and reduce it to nothingness, as if to show that we do not worship prowess. The ashes of the red heifer, when sprinkled on an individual who has come into contact with a corpse, takes away the *tum'ah* (ritual distancing) of that individual, who can then become ritually attached to the Temple service and other functions.

Since the red heifer is linked to the golden calf episode, the red heifer excerpt, once a year on a special occasion, is in reality read not in order to remind us of the red heifer. It is read in order to remind us of the golden calf episode. Just before the onset of the new spiritual calendar with the month of Nisan, we take stock. We read, and are subtly reminded, about an ignominious period in our history. Much as we would like to forget this part of our history, we are obliged to remember. This is clearly enunciated in the Torah, where the community is exhorted to "Remember, do not forget, how you provoked God. . ." (Devarim 9:7).

Why must we remember this dark episode, an episode that may be better forgotten? Because it is important for each individual to recognize that there is an inherent capacity to do wrong, and one must be ever alert to that possibility. We should never think that we are so good, or so virtuous, that we are incapable of behaving in an irresponsible or insensitive manner. By remembering the ignominy of the past, we reduce the possibility such ignominy will recur.

Within this background, it may be possible to better understand the juxtaposition of Shabbat Parah with Shabbat Zakhor. Just before Purim, we reiterate our commitment to eliminate evil from the world. Shortly after Purim, toward the end of the happy month of Adar, we reflect on ourselves. It is true that there is evil in the world. It is also wrong to assume that we, committed as we are to eliminating evil, are perfect. We too have failings, and these failings must be acknowledged. All too often, people, in their condemnation of others, fail to acknowledge their own failings. It is more convenient to blame others and, by blaming others, avoid confrontation with one's self.

The sages, by surrounding Purim with Zakhor and Parah, attempt to strike a delicate balance. Evil must be eliminated, but not at the expense of confrontation with one's self, with one's own failings. There is evil in the world that must be erased, but there is also the propensity for evil that exists in each one of us which we must face squarely. Hopefully, by facing this squarely, we will be well on the way toward eliminating it.

ḤANUKKAH
Balanced Perspective

The Talmud (Shabbat 21b), in discussing Ḥanukkah, makes little mention of the war fought by the Maccabees. The talmudic discussion is mostly about the miracle of the oil. On the other hand, in both the grace after meals and the *Amidah* (main prayer), in the text of *Al HaNisim*, which refers to the great Ḥanukkah miracle, the oil is mentioned only at the end. Even then, it is only mentioned in passing—that the people lit the oil. There is no mention of the fact that the oil lasted miraculously for eight days. The text is more concerned with the military battle that preceded Ḥanukkah. Why is there such a disparity between the Talmud and the liturgy concerning Ḥanukkah?

The Talmud addresses itself to the question of the ultimate significance of Ḥanukkah. Military battles have been too frequent in history to justify having a celebration just for victory in combat. Additionally, we avoid celebrating military victories. The only celebration that is institutionalized is the aftermath of the military victory, if that aftermath is peace and tranquility. It is the peace and tranquility that is celebrated.

With Ḥanukkah, more than peace and tranquility is celebrated. Of great significance is the fact that God gave the final stamp of approval to the entire process of return, through the miracle of the oil. This enabled the people to keep the light of the Temple burning, so that the *Bet HaMikdash* would be open to the community. It was God's way of endorsing the cause and the sincerity with which the campaign was fought. It also gave a spiritual thrust to the postwar reality. This inspired people who had previously been on the brink of assimilation to make a significant return to their roots.

On the other hand, the *Al HaNisim* prayer in the *Amidah* is in the section of thanksgiving. Here we give thanks to God for the great deliverance. The military deliverance was in fact an extraordinary feat. The handful of Maccabees fought against great odds, and by all military calculations should have been soundly defeated. But not only were they not defeated, they actually emerged victorious and able to rededicate the Temple. *Al HaNisim* gives thanks to God for enabling the Maccabees to overcome the tremendous obstacles that stood in their way.

But the key to establishing Hanukkah as a period of celebration is the fact that the people apprehended the moment as a call to return. This was their correct interpretation of the miraculous deliverance, an interpretation that was given the stamp of approval by God in the form of the miracle. The stamp of approval from God need not be singled out for a special thanks to God, since this was God's way of thanking the people for returning to the fold. It therefore does not belong in the *Amidah*, but it is the focal point of discussion when contemplating the question, What is Hanukkah?

The deliverance prior to Hanukkah and the return to traditional roots on Hanukkah itself speak of the ongoing partnership between God and Israel. It is a partnership which at times might be shaky, but thankfully has always endured.

PURIM
Is Purim Modeled after Pesaḥ?

The festive period of Purim is marked by a number of distinctive observances. The day prior to Purim is the Fast of Esther, unless Purim commences on Saturday night. In that case, the Fast of Esther is commemorated on the preceding Thursday. On Purim itself, the Megillah is read. We are obligated to celebrate Purim with a lavish feast, to send gifts to the poor (at least two poor people), and to send various types of food stuffs to at least one other individual (*mishloaḥ manot*).

Purim observances differ significantly from those of Ḥanukkah, whose major commemorations are the kindling of the Menorah and the recitation of *Hallel*. Though we take the specific Purim observances as almost an automatic reflex, it would be useful to ascertain why and how these modes of observance were established for the celebration of Purim.

The first possible clue to how they evolved may be detected in the talmudic observation that the original Fast of Esther, which took place immediately following Esther's becoming aware of the evil decrees, lasted three days. The final day of that fast was the first day of Pesaḥ (Talmud, Megillah 15a). The liberation of the Jewish community from Haman's machinations actually began on Pesaḥ, when Esther made her first approach to the king. Is it therefore farfetched to suggest that Mordekhai and his colleagues modeled Purim, to some extent, after Passover? If this is indeed the case, then the mode of observance associated with Purim follows a very distinctive pattern.

The major theme of Purim is the story of deliverance. We are obliged to tell the story of this deliverance just as we are obliged to tell the story of the Exodus from Egypt. On Purim the story is told by reading the Megillah; the Megillah is Purim's Haggadah.

On Pesaḥ we are asked to relive the actual events, to experience firsthand the new reality effected by Pesaḥ, namely, freedom. Thus we make significant changes to enhance the celebration of freedom.

Once Haman's decree became public, the Jewish community was unable to rejoice or to party. Because their lives were imperiled, celebrative events were out of the question. It therefore stands to reason that on Purim itself the people should commemorate their deliverance by doing that which they could not do previously, namely celebrating with a glorious feast.

However, in the same way as we experience the bitterness of servitude through storytelling and through eating bitter herbs on Pesaḥ night, we experience the sense of emergency and the peril of the people through fasting on the day prior to Purim. The fast, which is called the Fast of Esther in deference to Esther's major role, is not on the same day as Esther's three-day fast. Instead, it is a reliving of the dread which we assume the Jewish community experienced in anticipation of the enemy's attack—a dread surely marked by fasting and praying for deliverance. So, just as on Passover the bitterness precedes the freedom, so with Purim the fasting precedes the feasting.

Attendant to the obligation of feasting is the requirement that we give gifts to the poor and food stuffs to at least one other individual. The purpose of this is to allow the poor to purchase what is necessary for the Purim festivity and to assist at least one other individual with food and drink to help celebrate Purim properly.

This is reminiscent of but not identical to the practices observed on Pesah. On Pesah too we share with others, but in a different way. On Pesah, we urge all those who are in need to join us. The doors of the home are opened and anyone who is poor or who needs the companionship of the seder is asked to join. On Purim, however, there is no obligation to open the door. Instead we take from our home and send it to the homes of others. If Purim is to follow the model of Pesah, why was it suggested that the food be sent, rather than requiring people to host others, to have the poor as their guests for Purim?

It may be that the sages of that period, recognizing that much of the difficulty facing the community came from excessive partying, refused to encourage such behavior in the future. If open house partying were the norm, matters could easily get out of control. Instead of a spiritually sensitive celebration, the partying would be wild and uncontrolled.

Therefore, the method chosen for the Purim celebration was to help every other individual in the community and to hold smaller celebrations in individual homes. In the individual home, the individual chooses how to celebrate and is not dependent upon the choices others might make. Helping others to celebrate by sending them the food allows feasting to take place in more homes than would be the case if the poor were to be invited to major feasts instead. The partying was thus given a sense of proportion and meaning.

On balance, it does not seem at all farfetched that the Purim observances are modeled after those of Pesah. The departures from the Pesah pattern are necessary to maintain the true significance and purpose of the celebration. On Pesah we celebrate freedom; on Purim we rejoice in the freedom to celebrate.

IN-DEPTH STUDIES

THE SELLING OF THE BIRTHRIGHT
Making Sense of a Perplexing Episode

The selling of the birthright by Esau to Yaakov is one of the more perplexing episodes in the Torah. It raises many questions, not the least of which is the question of Yaakov's motivation in wresting this title from Esau. The relevant verses are found in Bereshit (25:29-34):

> 29. Yaakov let a dish simmer, and Esau came in from the field and he was faint.
> 30. Said Esau to Yaakov: Give me to devour, please, of this red red pottage, for I am faint; therefore he called his name Edom.
> 31. Said Yaakov: Sell to me, as this day, your birthright.
> 32. Said Esau: Behold I am going to die, what use then is this birthright to me?
> 33. Said Yaakov: Swear to me as this day, and he swore unto him, and he sold his birthright to Yaakov.
> 34. Then Yaakov gave Esau bread and a pottage of lentils, and he ate and he drank, stood up and went on his way; and Esau heaped contempt on the birthright.

There are some striking anomalies in the episode that merit some reflection.

First, why was Yaakov making a pottage? This certainly does not seem to be the role or obligation of the child, considering that, according to the Talmud (Baba Batra 16b), Yaakov and Esau were at the time only fifteen years old. This is slightly out of the ordinary, to say the least.

Second, when Esau asks, in desperation, to be given some of this pottage to eat, Yaakov immediately responds with the request that he be sold the birthright. There is no feeling of sorrow expressed that his twin brother is hungry and faint, only a cold, detached demand for the birthright. Is this the normal reaction that one would have to a request from his own brother?

Why did it even enter into Yaakov's mind that he should raise the subject of the birthright? This is certainly unusual and is not an exemplary model of behavior. In brotherly love, we think of people helping each other without looking for recompense or seeking to gain advantage from having helped. On the surface at least, Yaakov does not seem to follow in this tradition of brotherly love.

Finally, the episode concludes with the statement that Esau heaped contempt on the birthright. He had already heaped contempt earlier, before he ate, most significantly in verse 32, when he said, ". . . I am going to die, what use then is this birthright to me?" Why is the statement about his contemptuous attitude to the birthright left to the very end?

Perspective on this episode is best gained through an appreciation of two matters: (1) the significance of birthright at that time and (2) the financial condition in the household of Yizḥak and Rivkah, the parents of Yaakov and Esau.

It is a standard biblical principle that the firstborn male receives a double portion of the inheritance. Yet Ramban expresses doubt that this rule operated in the time of Yaakov and Esau. However, it is reasonable to assume that the firstborn did have specific responsibilities, which would justify receipt of a greater share of the inheritance.

These responsibilities would have included looking after the younger children and looking after the parents when they were no longer able to look after themselves. The firstborn was to a certain extent a buffer between the parents and the other children.

The firstborn was a child to the parents but a parentlike figure to the rest of the family.

The firstborn thus would have assumed the mantle of leadership within the family context. Under normal circumstances, the firstborn would have been the one most identified with the spiritual values of the family.

Insofar as the financial conditions of the family are concerned, Ibn Ezra (Bereshit 25:34) suggests that at that time, Yizḥak and Rivkah were quite poor. Although Ramban takes strong issue with Ibn Ezra on this matter, none of the questions with which he challenges Ibn Ezra's assertion are so strong as to defy any retort. It is possible that all the wealth that Yizḥak was given by his father Avraham may have been lost.

Why would Esau sell his birthright for a pottage if there was food aplenty in the household? It would seem as if there was very little food. Esau's desperation was accentuated by the fact that this may have been the only food available to him at the time. Ibn Ezra raises other questions. Why was it that when Yaakov was sent away from the house to escape the wrath of Esau later on, he was sent without any provisions or money, and had to entreat God for food and clothing (Bereshit 28:20). Ramban, in response to Ibn Ezra's claim, suggests that in fact provisions were given to Yaakov, but not in abundance, so as not to attract bandits on the way. With all this, midrashic commentary has it that Yaakov was robbed on the way.

Clearly, however, the suggestion that Yizḥak had become poor is certainly not beyond credibility. This would go a long way toward explaining the reality of the situation as it unfolded in this birthright episode.

Yaakov making a pottage is perhaps slightly unusual, but this may have projected his assumption of responsibility for taking care of family needs. If indeed the family was poor, Yaakov took it upon himself to help in the family situation through contributing his little bit; alleviating the burden on his parents by helping make lunch or supper.

At the same time that Yaakov took these responsibilities quite seriously, his brother Esau, not nearly as beholden to the family, was having a good time in the field. The setting for the situation is thus set with this very innocent verse (29): "Yaakov let a dish simmer, and Esau came in from the field and he was faint." He had enjoyed himself, spending a day in the field. The Torah does not say that he was tilling in the field or working the field; it just reports that he "came in from the field." This glaring omission suggests quite strongly that Esau was in the field just for a good time. The faint Esau then understandably asks Yaakov for the pottage. Yaakov's reaction, as reported in verse 31, is to ask for the birthright.

What at first glance seems to be a request coming from nowhere, now begins to make more sense. If in fact the responsibility of the firstborn is to look after the family needs and to assert leadership when leadership needs to be asserted, then it should have been Esau who was making the pottage for the family. Instead, he abdicated the leadership role that belongs to the firstborn and left it for Yaakov to fulfill. Meanwhile, he enjoyed life to the full.

Yaakov was understandably upset with this reversal of roles, and said to Esau, in so many words: If you want this role reversal to continue, if you want me to make the food for you and feed you, then at least acknowledge this officially. At least come out in the open and say that you no longer want the responsibilities that are incumbent upon the firstborn, and that you hereby acknowledge that I (Yaakov) have these responsibilities, and obviously all the advantages that pertain thereto.

Since Yizḥak was poor, it mattered little to Esau whether a firstborn would have any preferential treatment in the inheritance. Two times nothing is nothing. Any advantage that would have been coming to him by virtue of his being the firstborn was totally neutralized by the bad financial situation in which Yizḥak was mired. Feeling that the responsibilities and prerogatives of the firstborn were a burden without any material advantage,

Esau was ready to sell his birthright for whatever benefit he might gain.

But perhaps this pejorative judgment is a bit unfair. After all, Esau was desperately hungry at this time. It is possible to see his willingness to sell the birthright as a reflection of the desperate nature of his situation. The text (verse 34) tells us that this is not so. After Yaakov gave Esau what he had requested—and even more, including bread and the pottage of lentils—and he ate and drank, Esau simply got up and left. With his desperate plight alleviated and his hunger satisfied, Esau could have spent some time contemplating the reality of his relationship with his brother. He could have wondered whether it was wise to abdicate his responsibilities, and he could have expressed regret to his brother. He could have said: Yaakov, what you have been doing until now is really my responsibility. I realize that I have unfairly removed myself from this and it has fallen on your shoulders. This experience has awakened me to the aberration in my behavior, and from now on I would like to behave in a manner befitting the firstborn.

But Esau said nothing; he just got up and left. His failure to contemplate the implications and repercussions of his actions leads the Torah to say, "and Esau heaped contempt on the birthright." His unwillingness to make amends even after the emergency had disappeared was the ultimate show of contempt. Esau thus showed that he wanted nothing of the leadership role in the family; he only wanted to enjoy himself.

It was, therefore, eminently fair, and in fact necessary, for Yaakov to hear the official acknowledgment from Esau of his ill-advised decision to renounce family responsibility, in order that Yaakov would know that the firstborn's responsibility now became his.

It is important to understand this episode in its entirety, related as it is to the complex realities that prevailed within the household, because it is upon this that much of ensuing Israelite history is based. With this understanding, one can hardly suggest that Esau was given a raw deal or that he was cheated. If anything, it is he who through his irresponsible behavior caused the birthright roles to be reversed.

For Esau to have later expected that his father, Yizḥak, would bless him and bestow upon him the mantle of family leadership was, and remains, an instance of unbridled, first-class ḥutzpah.

REACTION TO TERROR
A Biblical Perspective

Over the course of the past few decades, the free world has been in the grip of terrorism. Terrorists have been free to roam the Western world and to hold Western civilization hostage as they attack innocent people, murder and assassinate indiscriminately, and hijack ordinary citizens who are on routine travel.

Affected governments have boasted about their commitment to fight terrorism and to beat it, but their rhetoric has certainly not been matched by effective action. The question of how to behave in a civilized fashion against brutality and animal behavior has yet to be answered.

This short excursus into a biblical scenario examines what may be the first strategic approach to hostage taking and might serve as a partial guide to the contemporary situation.

> When the Canaanite, the King of Arad, who dwelt in the Negev, learned that Israel was coming by the way of Atarim, he engaged Israel in battle and took of them captives. Then Israel made a vow to God and said, "If you deliver these people into our hand, we will utterly destroy their towns." God heeded Israel's plea and delivered up the Canaanites, and they and their cities were utterly destroyed; so that place was named Ḥormah [implying utter destruction]. (Be-midbar 21:1-3)

At first glance, this seems to be a case of captives taken during the course of battle. However, if we examine the text carefully we see that the phrase "he engaged Israel in battle" indicates that it was a one-sided conflict. The king of Arad heard that Israel was coming by the way of Atarim. Israel was merely in the midst of a journey. They had no intention to do battle, they had no military pretensions. They were merely going on a trip to a destination. They were attacked by the Canaanite king and his people, in what was a declaration of war by the Canaanites. But it was a one-sided declaration. They ventured to attack Israel for no reason, without provocation.

It is worth noting that the king of Arad is identified (Midrash Rabbah, Be-midbar 19:20) with Amalek. Amalek is, of course, the archenemy of Israel, the group of murderers who sought to destroy Israel immediately after the Exodus from Egypt. The Amalekites are now dressed up as Canaanites, or as decent-looking people who camouflaged their terrorism by pretending to belong to a respected nation. Herein is revealed one of the difficulties in dealing with terrorism. Terrorists wear differing clothing at different times in order to suit their own interests. Because of this they are a difficult target to pinpoint and attack with accuracy.

The biblical text goes on to say that in their warring against Israel, the Canaanites succeeded in taking captives. The more precise translation would be hostages, not captives, since Israel did not make war against Canaan but was attacked wantonly. Rashi states that the Canaanites succeeded in taking exactly one hostage, one maidservant. Ramban seems to indicate that the simple meaning of the text would point to their having taken a number of hostages, rather than just one. Whatever the number, Israel's reaction to this hostage taking becomes a matter of contemporary moment.

Israel was obviously concerned with this turn of events, and refused to sit by idly as a hostage was taken, or hostages. Israel approached God with the following proposition: "If you deliver this people into our hand, we will utterly destroy their towns"

(Be-midbar 21:2). This proposition made by Israel to God is problematic. Israel was faced with a crisis. Its immediate objective should have been the freeing of the hostage or hostages. Instead, Israel asks for the deliverance of Canaan into their hands, at which time they will utterly destroy the Canaanites' towns. Why the need to destroy the towns, and why the complicated request to God? Why not a simple request, "Please, God, help us succeed in defeating this enemy and freeing our hostages"?

Israel realized the implications of what was transpiring. This was an assault on innocents, on a vulnerable people that was making a long trek toward its home. It was therefore not merely sufficient that they be victorious in combat. The situation demanded that they respond with such ferocity and overwhelming force that no group would ever again dare to attack them and take innocent people away to be used as leverage.

Israel thus asked God to ensure their military victory, after which they would utterly destroy the towns. The text uses the word *v'haharamti* to signify utter destruction. It is derived from the word "*herem*," which, Rashi explains, indicates dedicating all of the spoils to God. Israel was not out to gain any booty; it was out to teach a lesson. That lesson was utter destruction, with all the spoils being dedicated to God. This was to impart a message from on high to all nations that would contemplate attacking Israel. They should think twice, because the consequences that await them are the same consequences that were visited upon the Canaanites.

It is instructive that Israel did not send any warnings to the Canaanites, telling them what they intended to do if the hostages were not returned. At least, we have no record of such a message being sent. Instead of making statements, pious platitudes which perhaps could not be kept, Israel pleaded for God's intervention to allow them to succeed. They proceeded to do what they had to in order to protect their vulnerable populace. Israel took action, and let that action do its own talking.

From the third verse, we learn that Israel was indeed successful. They defeated the Canaanites, and, as Ramban indicates, they were able to return the hostages safely and to utterly destroy the Canaanite towns, so much so that the place itself was called "utter destruction," or Ḥormah.

From this biblical hostage-taking incident, one can derive a number of principles.

1. There is no difference between one hostage and one hundred hostages. The reaction to one must be the same as the reaction to many. If one is willing to forgo the fate of a single person, then eventually one will be oblivious to the fate of the multitude.

2. The reaction to the incident must be free of empty rhetoric that cannot be acted upon. It is probably better not to say anything and just take action.

3. The reaction, militarily, of necessity takes into account the possibility that the hostages may become victims. But that cannot be allowed to deter from a swift response, since negotiating with evil only legitimizes evil.

4. The reaction to the hostage taking should not conform to any rules of commensurateness. Overkill is a legitimate option. In other words, Israel, or any victimized nation or country, need not restrict itself to a limited operation that, because of its limited nature, effectively compromises the response. Instead, it is perfectly permissible, even logical and desirable, to declare total war on the terrorist group and to utterly destroy it. This is not for vengeance; it is to ensure that one's people can live in safety. A blow so severe remains an eternal deterrent to those who would chance such a venture in the future.

Of course, the contemporary reaction to terrorism has been neither swift nor overwhelming. It is obvious that the situation today may be different from the situation in biblical times, but the biblical model is nevertheless useful in suggesting the types of effective political and military action that can and should be taken to erase this international menace.

THE RATIONALE FOR SACRIFICE
A Postscript on Abravanel's Defense of Rambam

The controversy concerning the rationale for sacrifice offered by Rambam is well known. The difficulties relate to consistency and validity. Regarding consistency, the difficulty inheres in reconciling Rambam's view of sacrifice as it appears in his classic work *Mishneh Torah* and his rationale for sacrifice as it appears in his philosophical work *Guide for the Perplexed*. In *Mishneh Torah* Rambam ennobles sacrifice as a primary eternal mode of spiritual expression. Regarding validity, the difficulty centers around the rationale offered in the *Guide*; specifically, the very validity of the rationale as legitimization for the sacrificial order. The matter of reconciling the apparently diverse views of Rambam is linked to the question of what is the relationship between the *Guide* and the *Mishneh Torah*.

The rationale itself came under fierce attack from Ramban in his commentary on the Torah. The contentious argument of Rambam is contained in the latter part of the *Guide for the Perplexed* (III, 32):

> For a sudden transition from one opposite to another is impossible. And therefore man, according to his nature, is not capable of abandoning suddenly all to which he was accustomed . . . and as at that time the way of life generally accepted and customary in the whole world and the universal service upon which we were brought up

> consisted in offering various species of living beings in the temples in which images were set up, in worshipping the latter, and in burning incense before them—the pious ones and the ascetics being at that time, as we have explained, the people who were devoted to the service of the temples consecrated to the stars: His wisdom, may He be exalted, and His gracious ruse, which is manifest in regard to all His creatures, did not require that He give us a Law prescribing the rejection, abandonment, and abolition of all these kinds of worship. For one could not then conceive the acceptance of [such a Law], considering the nature of man, which always likes that to which it is accustomed. At that time this would have been similar to the appearance of a prophet in these times who, calling upon the people to worship God, would say: "God has given you a Law forbidding you to pray to Him, to fast, to call upon Him for help in misfortune. Your worship should consist solely in meditation without any works at all." Therefore He, may He be exalted, suffered the above-mentioned kinds of worship to remain, but transferred them from created or imaginary and unreal things to His own name, may He be exalted, commanding us to practice them with regard to Him, may He be exalted.

Rambam goes on to elaborate that through this Divine "ruse," idolatry was effectively effaced and a foundation of Judaic belief firmly established, even at the very time that the people were not turned away through the abolition of the worship modes to which they had become accustomed.

Why could God not have given us a law which would reveal the first intention and simultaneously give us the capacities to actualize that law? Rambam shows that sacrifices were not the only instances wherein God's actions related directly to the human condition; more precisely, to what could be expected from the people in their present condition. He cites as an example the path taken by the Israelites in the Exodus from Egypt. The people were not ready to proceed, immediately following prolonged servitude, to the challenges that would face them. They wandered in the desert until they became courageous enough to face the challenges; the desert being a place where, owing to the lack of normal comforts, one necessarily develops courage. The same dynamics were at work in the order of sacrifices.

Insofar as the capacity of God to change human nature and to bring it to a level of receptivity, Rambam, whilst affirming the capacity of God to do this, rejects such a contingency. If God were to intervene in this manner, the giving of the Law would be useless. This is seemingly an argument for unencumbered free will on the part of human beings. This, in capsule form, is the position advanced by Rambam.

Ramban, in his commentary on the Torah, vehemently rejects the rationale offered by Rambam (Va-yikra 1:9). He calls this rationale vain talk which pollutes the table of God, in claiming that sacrifice was only established to detract from the wicked and fools of the world, when Scripture indicates that this is an offering which is a sweet savor unto God. God forbid that there should be no value to the sacrifices save to negate idolatry.

A careful reading of Rambam indicates that he does not suggest the negation of idolatry as the sole reason for the sacrifices. The sacrifices were motivated by a recognition that without sacrifice, the people would veer toward idolatry. Once having implemented sacrifice for this reason, the sacrifices themselves take on a transcending purpose, what is referred to by Rambam as the realization of God's first intention.

Abravanel, in his introduction to Va-yikra, defends Rambam against the attack of Ramban. He refers to Rambam's argument that in fact prayer, supplication, and fasting are more consistent with God's first intention and therefore are valid expressions in all places, at all times. On the other hand, sacrifices are restricted both in time and place, as well as in who is authorized to offer the sacrifices. This would seem to be an indication that prayer is universal and sacrifice more limited. Additionally, the oft-heard prophetic harangues against people who put all their eggs in the

The Rationale for Sacrifice / 187

sacrificial basket, but do not heed God's word, indicate the primariness of the relationship with God, with sacrifice being secondary, and merely a means to an end.

Abravanel cites a midrash which seemingly correlates with the approach of Rambam:

> R. Pinḥas in the name of R. Levi said: The matter may be compared to the case of a king's son who thought he could do what he liked and habitually ate the flesh of *nevelot* and *terefot*. Said the king: "I will have him always at my own table and he will automatically be hedged round." Similarly, because Israel were passionate followers after idolatry in Egypt and used to bring their sacrifices to the satyrs, as it is written, "And they shall no more sacrifice their sacrifices unto the satyrs" (Va-yikra 17:7)—and these satyrs are nought but demons, as is borne out by the text which says, "They sacrificed unto demons, no-gods" (Devarim 32:17), these demons being nought but satyrs, as it says, "And satyrs shall dance there" (Yeshayahu 13:21)—and they used to offer their sacrifices in the forbidden high places, on account of which punishments used to come upon them, the Holy One, blessed be He, said: "Let them offer their sacrifices to Me at all times in the Tent of Meeting, and thus they will be separated from idolatry and be saved from punishment." Hence it is written, Whichever man there be of the House of Israel that killed an ox . . . and has not brought it unto the door of the Tent of Meeting, etc.

The weight of evidence from Scripture and rabbinic sources leads Abravanel to conclude that Rambam's thesis is not vain talk, as was asserted by Ramban. Instead, Rambam's thesis is holy talk.

The defence of Rambam by Abravanel is even more interesting in that Abravanel seemingly adopts the central thesis of Rambam in explaining a difficult scriptural portion in Devarim (27:2—8):

2. And it shall be on the day when you shall pass over the Jordan unto the land which the Lord your God gives you that you shall set great stones, and plaster them with plaster.

3. And you shall write upon them all the words of this Law, when you are passed over; that you may go in unto the land which the Lord your God gives you, a land flowing with milk and honey, as the Lord, the God of your fathers, has promised you.

4. And it shall be when you are passed over the Jordan, that you shall set up these stones, which I command you this day, in Mount Eval, and you shall plaster them with plaster.

5. And there shall you build an altar unto the Lord your God, an altar of stones; you shall lift up no iron tool upon them.

6. You shall build the altar of the Lord your God of unhewn stones; and you shall offer burnt offerings thereon unto the Lord your God.

7. And you shall sacrifice peace-offerings, and shall eat there; and you shall rejoice before the Lord your God.

8. And you shall write upon the stones all the words of this law very plainly.

Abravanel, in his commentary on these verses, addresses himself to a host of problems. Verses 2 and 3 speak about setting up great stones and writing on them the words of the Law, but this seems to be repeated again for no apparent reason in verses 4 and 8. There are other problems with repetition in the verses which Abravanel addresses, but they are not central to the issue concerning us in this discussion.

Abravanel resolves this issue by alluding to the practice of conquering armies to set up signs on the road or at the gate of a city in the name of their leader in celebration of the victory of the conquering forces, giving the dates and details of the great event. Verses 2 and 3 are therefore not part of a commandment. Instead they are an expression of what would be realistically expected of the people. It would be expected of them that upon entering the land of Israel, they, like other conquering forces, would set up great stones and write details of their victory upon them. They would write the story of their having passed over into the Land of Israel and the reason for doing so, that they were coming into the land given to them by God. According to Abravanel's understanding, verses 2 and 3 would read as follows:

> 2. And it shall be on the day when you shall pass over the Jordan unto the land which the Lord your God gives you, that you will set up great stones, and plaster them with plaster.
>
> 3. And you will write upon them the story of your passing over because you will have gone into the land which the Lord your God gives you. . .

Verse 4 begins a commentary on the anticipated actions spelled out in verses 2 and 3. Assuming that you will naturally, like other peoples, set up the stones and celebrate the event, you are hereby being told that you should set up the stones not in the way that others have done it, but in a unique fashion. The commandment, therefore, begins with verse 4, and prescribes a mitzvah content to an anticipated act. The mitzvah involves transcending the natural nationalistic expressions of other peoples and making this expression a glorification of God, as indicated in verses 6 and 7. After glorifying God on the altar of stone, the altar should be taken apart and the stones placed in foundation. On the stones were to be written not merely the story of the crossing, but also the entire Torah with its commandments.

Abravanel's explanation of this difficult series of scriptural verses is remarkably consistent with, if not an almost exact paraphrase of, Rambam's rationale for sacrifice. The desire to place stones celebrating the great event of conquest is a conditioned reaction related to a prevailing norm, as indeed is the rite of sacrifice. The rite of sacrifice was not abolished, as that would have caused too much tension and turmoil within the people. Instead, through a set of restrictive parameters, the act of sacrifice was exalted and ennobled to serve a godly purpose. Similarly, the act of setting up stones was not abolished, in recognition of the people's legitimate desire to celebrate the event of their entry into Israel. Instead, the act itself was given sanction and sanctity by changing it from an egotistical celebration of human actions into a celebration of God's glory and power. Abravanel's interpretation more than reinforces Rambam's rationale for sacrifice. It actually incorporates that rationale into the biblical framework.

Emanating from the thesis of Rambam and the exegesis of Abravanel is the proposition that the Torah is a Divine document addressed to the human condition with all its frailties. It may be that ultimately such observances as the sacrificial rite become statute, as Rambam himself indicates. But the statute dimension is the higher one, and it can only be reached by stepping into the observance on the more mundane level of detachment from either idolatry or vain expression.

Rav's view that "the precepts were given for the express purpose of purifying mankind" (Midrash Rabbah, Bereshit 44:1), is an indication that the Torah is seen as the initiator and actualizer of a process. The *Guide* addresses itself to the launching of this process; the *Mishneh Torah* addresses itself to its ultimate purpose.

APPLICABILITY INDEX

The subjects covered in this volume relate mainly to specific Torah readings or special occasions. Many themes, however, relate to more than one Torah reading and may also be useful for other special occasions. This index lists the Torah readings and special topics in the order they appear in the book and suggests further possible applications for each discussion.

Bereshit—Bo, Israel, Kedoshim.
Noaḥ—caring.
Lekh Lekha—decency in religion, respecting parents.
Va-yera—rejecting evil.
Ḥayyei Sarah—true love, wedding.
Toledot—deservedness.
Va-yeẓe—Israel, Ki Tavo, moral values.
Va-yishlaḥ—protecting family.
Va-yeshev—Jewish history.
Mi-keẓ—anti-Semitism, Va-yeḥi.
Va-yiggash—parenting, Shema.
Va-yeḥi—caring for parents, fairness, Mi-keẓ.
Shemot—Messianism.
Va-era—old age.
Bo—Pesaḥ.
Be-shallaḥ—anti-Semitism.
Yitro—humility, Shavuot, Va-etḥannan.
Mishpatim—conjugal union, parental responsibility.

Terumah—authentic human relations, wedding.
Teẓavveh—chosenness, responsibility.
Ki Tissa—Purim, Shabbat Shekalim, unity.
Va-yakhel—charity, fund-raising.
Ẓav—guilt, thoughts.
Tazri'a—Bar Mitzvah, circumcision, child rearing, Emor, marital happiness, pain.
Meẓora—humility, Pesaḥ, return to Judaism.
Aḥarei Mot—homosexuality.
Kedoshim—Bereshit, love, Shemini-Atzeret, wedding.
Emor—divorce, Tazria, therapy.
Be-har—Pesaḥ, purpose, Shavuot.
Be-ḥukkotai—ecology, reward.
Be-midbar—fertility, rising to challenge or crisis, Shemot.
Naso—adultery, substance abuse.
Be-ha'alotkha—envy, Jewish history, pride.
Shelaḥ—Israel, language, women.
Koraḥ—honor, rebellion.
Ḥukkat—medicine, Shabbat Parah.
Balak—anti-Semitism, delegitimizing.
Pinḥas—gratitude, Israel.
Mattot—leadership, unity.
Masei—gratitude.
Devarim—education, leadership.
Va-etḥannan—destiny, health preservation, Ki Teẓe, Shavuot, Ve-zot Ha-berakhah.
Ekev—Israel, obstinacy.
Re'eh—mourning, unity.
Shofetim—having a Torah, leadership.
Ki Teẓe—ecology, honoring parents, Shavuot, Va-etḥannan.
Ki Tavo—gratitude, Pesaḥ, Va-yeẓe.
Niẓavim—substance abuse.
Va-yelekh—education, Simḥat Torah, Sukkot, unity.
Ha'azinu—generation gap, ingratitude.
Ve-zot Ha-berakhah—Be-ha'alotkha, Torah lifting, Va-etḥannan.

Rosh Ha-Shanah—pain, parenting, Va-yera.
Yom Kippur—collective guilt, guilt.
Pesaḥ—education, Ki Tavo, Lekh Lekha.
Shavuot—freedom, Mishpatim, Yitro.
Sukkot—inner beauty, joy, Va-yelekh.
Shemini Atzeret-Simḥat Torah—Kedoshim, looking Jewish.
Zakhor and Parah—anti-Semitism, Purim.

SUBJECT INDEX

This index is listed according to topic. Each topic is followed by the Sidrah, Yom Tov, and special occasion presentations in which the topic is discussed. Sidrah or Yom Tov topics contained in other Sidrah presentations are also found in the list of topics.

Adultery—Naso.
Anti-Semitism—Balak, Be-shallaḥ, Mi-keẓ, Zakhor and Parah.
Authentic human relations—Terumah.
Bar Mitzvah—Tazri'a.
Be-ha'alothkha—Ve-zot Ha-berakhah.
Bereshit—Bo, Kedoshim.
Bo—Bereshit.
Caring—Noaḥ.
Caring for parents—Va-yeḥi.
Charity—Va-yakhel.
Child rearing—Tazri'a.
Chosenness—Teẓavveh.
Circumcision—Tazri'a.
Collective guilt—Yom Kippur.
Conjugal union—Mishpatim.
Delegitimizing—Balak
Decency in religion—Lekh Lekha.
Deservedness—Toledot.
Divorce—Emor.

Ecology—Be-ḥukkotai, Ki Teẓe.
Education—Devarim, Pesaḥ, Va-yelekh.
Emor—Tazria.
Envy—Be-ha'alothkha
Fairness—Va-yeḥi.
Fertility—Be-midbar.
Freedom—Shavuot.
Fund-raising—Va-yakhel.
Generation gap—Ha'azinu.
Gratitude—Ki Tavo, Masei, Pinḥas. .
Guilt—Yom Kippur, Ẓav.
Having a Torah—Shofetim.
Health preservation—Va-etḥannan.
Homosexuality—Aḥarei Mot.
Honor—Koraḥ.
Honoring parents—Ki Teẓe.
Humility—Meẓora, Yitro.
Ignoring responsibility—Va-yikra.
Ingratitude—Ha'azinu.
Inner beauty—Sukkot.
Israel—Bereshit, Ekev, Pinḥas, Shelaḥ, Va-yeẓe.
Jewish history—Be-ha'alotkha, Vayeshev.
Joy—Sukkot.
Kashrut—Shemini.
Kedoshim—Bereshit, Shemini Atzeret-Simḥat Torah.
Ki Teẓe—Shavuot, Va-etḥannan.
Ki Tavo—Va-yeẓe.
Kindness—Shemini.
Language—Shelaḥ.
Leadership—Devarim, Mattot, Shofetim.
Lekh Lekha—Pesaḥ.
Looking Jewish—Shemini Atzeret-Simḥat Torah.
Love—Kedoshim.
Marital happiness—Tazria.
Medicine—Ḥukkat.
Messianism—Shemot.

Mi-kez — Va-yeḥi.
Miracles — Ḥannukah.
Mishpatim — Shavuot.
Moral values — Va-yeze.
Mourning — Re'eh.
Neatness — Re'eh.
Obstinacy — Ekev.
Old age — Va-era.
Pain — Rosh Ha-Shanah, Tazria.
Parental responsibility — Mishpatim.
Parenting — Rosh Ha-Shanah, Va-yiggash.
Pesaḥ — Be-har, Bo, Ki Tavo, Mezora, Pesaḥ.
Pride — Be-ha'alothkha.
Protecting family — Va-yishlaḥ.
Purim — Ki Tissa, Pesaḥ, Zakhor and Parah.
Purpose — Be-har.
Rebellion — Koraḥ.
Rejecting evil — Va-yera.
Reliving — Purim.
Respecting parents — Lekh Lekha.
Responsibility — Tezavveh.
Return to Judaism — Mezora.
Reward — Be-ḥukkotai.
Rising to challenge or crisis — Be-midbar.
Shabbat Parah — Ḥukkat.
Shabbat Shekalim — Ki Tissa.
Shavuot — Be-har, Ki Teze, Va-ethannan, Yitro.
Shema — Va-yiggash.
Shemot — Be-midbar.
Simḥat Torah — Va-yelekh.
Steadfastness — Pekudei.
Substance abuse — Naso, Nizavim.
Sukkot — Va-yelekh.
Tazria — Emor.
Therapy — Emor.
Thoughts — Zav.

Torah lifting—Ve-zot Ha-Berakhah.
True love—Ḥayyei Sarah.
Unity—Ki Tissa, Mattot, Re'eh, Va-yelekh.
Va-ethannan—Ki Teẓe, Yitro.
Va-yeḥi—Mi-keẓ
Va-yera—Rosh Ha-Shanah.
Va-yeẓe—Ki Tavo.
Victory—Ḥannukah, Purim
Wedding—Ḥayyei Sarah, Kedoshim, Terumah.
Welfare—Shemini.
Women—Shelaḥ.
Yitro—Shavuot.